Wills, death & taxes made simple

NOEL WHITTAKER

NWH

By the same author:

MAKING MONEY MADE SIMPLE
GETTING IT TOGETHER
GOLDEN RULES OF WEALTH
SHARES MADE SIMPLE
LOANS MADE SIMPLE
MONEY TIPS
RETIREMENT MADE SIMPLE
MORE MONEY WITH NOEL WHITTAKER
LIVING WELL IN RETIREMENT
CONTROLLING YOUR CREDIT CARDS
SUPERANNUATION MADE SIMPLE
SUPERANNUATION MADE EASY
25 YEARS OF WHITT & WISDOM
10 SIMPLE STEPS TO FINANCIAL FREEDOM

Co-authored

with Rachel Lane

AGED CARE, WHO CARES?
RETIREMENT LIVING HANDBOOK
DOWNSIZING MADE SIMPLE

with James Whittaker

THE BEGINNER'$ GUIDE TO WEALTH

with Julia Hartman

SAVING TAX ON YOUR INVESTMENT PROPERTY
WINNING PROPERTY TAX STRATEGIES

WILLS, DEATH & TAXES MADE SIMPLE
First published in Australia in 2024
Reprinted May 2024
Reprinted July 2024
Reprinted November 2024
Reprinted December 2025

Visit our website at ***www.noelwhittaker.com.au***

NATIONAL LIBRARY OF AUSTRALIA

A catalogue record for this book is available from the National Library of Australia

ISBN 978-0-6458216-4-2 (pbk)

Editing by Helena Bond
Cover design & typesetting by Sharon Felschow, dta studio
Cartoons by Paul Lennon
Printed in Australia by McPherson's Printing Group, Victoria

This book is dedicated to my readers who so generously shared their tales of caution and experience so that others may benefit and sleep easy.

About the author

International bestselling author, finance and investment expert, radio broadcaster, newspaper columnist, and public speaker, Noel Whittaker is one of the world's foremost authorities on personal finance.

Noel reaches over three million readers each week through his columns in major Australian newspapers in Sydney, Melbourne, Perth, and Brisbane. He is a contributor to various magazines and websites, and appears regularly on radio and television.

Noel is one of Australia's most successful authors, with more than 20 bestselling books achieving worldwide sales of more than two million copies. His first book, *Making Money Made Simple*, set Australian sales records and was named in the 100 Most Influential Books of the Twentieth Century.

In 2011, he was made a Member of the Order of Australia for service to the community in raising awareness of personal finance.

Noel is now an Adjunct Professor with the Queensland University of Technology and a member of the Australian Securities and Investments Commission (ASIC) consumer liaison committee.

Acknowledgements

Estate planning is a massive topic because it covers such a myriad of issues, many of which are uncertain. It's not just the interplay of important topics such as tax, superannuation and Centrelink — the estate planning laws differ from state to state. To this heady mix we add the many facets of human psychology. Many people just don't get around to making a will, and even if they do, there are the other challenges of choosing an executor and handling the competing interests of family members. There are further complications due to the number of people living longer and re-partnering later in life, and also the possibility of diminishing mental capacity.

And there's more — many people I know have children living overseas, and over 50% of Australians were born overseas or have a parent living overseas. This brings the complexity of overseas assets and overseas beneficiaries into play.

Nobody is a specialist in all these areas, and I have been privileged when writing this book to have had invaluable help from experts in their field. The estate planning side was overseen by Kirsty Mackie, a solicitor in private practice who practises in both estate planning and family law; the tax section was co-written with Julia Hartman, a tax specialist in foreign residency issues, capital gains tax and deceased estates; and my guiding light in the superannuation section was Meg Heffron, one of Australia's foremost authorities on superannuation. I was also privileged to receive valuable input from special counsel Barbara Houlihan, John Perri of AMP Technical, retired solicitor John McLaughlin, and barrister Don Fraser KC.

I am indebted to my wife, Geraldine, for spending many hours with me debating the content; my long-time editor Helena Bond, who always goes the extra mile; and my sounding board Colin Newton for advice on content and layout.

Special thanks to Sharon Felschow, who has been typesetting my books for 25 years — she is not only a talented designer but also committed to meeting deadlines with exceptional dedication. Paul Lennon has done a great job on the cartoons as always, and McPherson's, as usual, has taken care of the printing.

Thank you all for being on the team.

Contents

Introduction

Every year in Australia, millions of dollars are spent on legal fees, and hundreds of thousands of hours are wasted in family disputes — all because of poor estate planning. So much of this stress, wasted time and money could be avoided by getting your estate planning right from the start. It's not rocket science, but it does involve awareness of the ramifications of what you do, and getting first-class advice, if appropriate. This is a growth area: as the population grows, and people live longer, the amount of wealth held by older people will increase. I predict that in the coming decades, there will be even more fighting over estates, exacerbated by the growing number of law firms advertising "no win, no fee" in this area.

It's a sad indictment of our attitude to this important topic that almost 50% of Australians still die without a will. But it gets worse — apparently for those who do have a will, 70% of them don't know where it is, couldn't locate it easily if asked to, and haven't reviewed it in the past 20 years. This means it's most likely to be outdated and no longer reflect their current circumstances. There's also a common misconception that people don't need to make a will because their wife, husband, or partner will automatically get everything. This is not true.

An estate planning lawyer tells me the following types of conversations are all too common.

Q: Where is your will?

A: I don't know, with my solicitor / accountant / at home, I think.

Q: When did you make it?

A: Oh, when the kids were born / 30 years ago / when we lived in Melbourne/Sydney.

Q: Has anything changed since then?

A: Oh yes, we moved from interstate / our daughter has married/divorced / we lent our son $100,000 to go into business …

And, of course, if you die without a will, the outcomes for those you leave behind can be horrendous.

Every person over 18 should have a will, so why do so many people refrain from setting out an estate plan? Here's a list of common reasons people give for procrastinating over making a will.

If I die first, my partner will do the right thing and share the money evenly between the children.

But it doesn't always play out that way — even if they are totally trustworthy, if the surviving partner starts a new relationship a whole new set of dynamics opens up.

It's all too hard!

Many people don't want to face up to the issue of making their will because of possible conflicts within the family. There may be a loving and devoted daughter who is always there for the parents, and there may be a black sheep who is seen only at Christmas time. Other family members may sit in the middle. Let's face it, when you make a will you make choices. Blended families (the Brady Bunch syndrome) may have even more complex concerns, as may those with family members who can't manage their own affairs. If it means having a difficult conversation around who gets what, it may feel easier just to ignore it.

It's too expensive.

Others are put off by the cost (very much like being put off at the thought of paying for good financial advice). Why pay for a lawyer when I can get a will kit from the newsagency for $25!

Our children know what we want.

This is ignorant thinking, since super and life insurance (which apart from their home probably forms the bulk of their estate) don't automatically fall into their estate. The trustee of those assets, which could well be the management of a huge insurance company, rather than any of the children, may ultimately decide who receives them.

Why should I bother? It won't be my problem when I'm 6 feet under.

As you read this book, notice that there is a wide range of issues that may affect what you choose to do. Just keep in mind that we aim to provide you with some essential estate planning information so you will be better able to navigate the path to a good outcome. It's a complex topic, and the laws also vary from state to state. Therefore, at best, this book is a guide.

We also hope to show you that estate planning is about much more than having a will — we're talking about control over time, transfer of ownership, handling issues such as assets that may be held in trust, and incapacity. This is why an enduring power of attorney is also a critically important document.

This book is not a substitute for getting good advice (and good advice is worth paying for). All we can provide here is general information — basic knowledge that will give you the power to seek the advice you need — nothing can replace getting good input, specific to your own situation, from a solicitor, accountant, and financial adviser.

Getting going

Welcome to the world of estate planning! Getting your affairs in order is one of the most important jobs you can ever do. It gives you the opportunity to make sure the assets you worked so hard to acquire will flow on to those you wish to receive them. And by understanding how the tax laws work, you could save your beneficiaries a fortune in unnecessary tax. It is also one of the most loving things you can do for your family — inadequate estate planning has the potential to cause so much stress and heartbreak.

I'll cover all these in detail in this book, but you will need to understand a few fundamentals to start.

1. Estate planning laws vary from state to state, so the best I can do in this book is explain the basic principles which may help you to understand the steps you need to take next.
2. Not all assets can be disposed of by your will. Usually the person with the final say on who gets your superannuation is the trustee of your super fund. If property is owned in joint names, the survivor automatically gets it irrespective of the terms of the will.
3. People's circumstances may change regularly — the big four life changes are birth, death, marriage and divorce. This is why documents such as wills and powers of attorney should be regularly reviewed to make sure they are up-to-date and reflect changing circumstances and potentially changing laws. This means a minimum of every five years or upon the happening of a life-changing event.
4. It's wise to engage a range of professionals if your affairs are even a little complicated because they all have different skills, and it's important that they work together to ensure the best outcome for you. For example, an estate lawyer is the best person to advise on the structure of your will and other relevant documents, but your accountant and financial planner need to be involved to make sure the tax considerations are taken care of.

Remember, it's easier to get things right from the start than try to rewrite history when troubles emerge in the future. I am told that many clients think their matter is straightforward and just want a "simple, cheap will". However, once the solicitor starts asking some probing questions they realise there is more to it than just leaving everything to their partner.

5. Understand the importance of getting the paperwork right and having it readily accessible. Far too much time and money are wasted because of incomplete, inappropriate or missing documents. Don't get caught in that trap. This is not as simple as it sounds as it's not always a quick process. People often start off in a flurry of enthusiasm but then lose interest halfway through, or decide to finish it off after they get back from a holiday. Of course, life gets in the way and they never get around to doing it, or tragedy strikes in the meantime.

6. Because of the frailties of human nature, disputes and litigation are extremely common in this field. As a result, the laws can change if a leading court case breaks new ground. This is why ongoing attention to your estate planning is necessary. Never forget the saying: "You never really know people until you've shared an inheritance with them."

Estates can bring out the ugly side in people, and death of a parent may also bring out family tensions between siblings and/or parents that have been lying dormant (but festering) for years. When mum or dad has passed, these tensions are spewed into the open.

Women in court fighting over will

Greg Stolz

A will war that erupted between two women over the estate of a slain Brisbane businessman has reached a ceasefire, with a secret settlement reached in court.

Concrete company boss Khalil Ibrahim, 59, was stabbed and bludgeoned to death in October 2021 after going to employee Jordan van Doorn's Cannon Hill house to drop off his pay. Van Doorn, 31, was last year found guilty of Mr Ibrahim's frenzied murder, with the Supreme Court hearing how h used a wrench and kitche knife to bludgeon and stab h boss "many times".

Marisol Mabansag

Paula Hitchcock leaving court on Friday. Picture: Sam Ruttyn

Family fight for fortune goes on

Brenden Hills

The love child of late billionaire Richard Pratt received three payments from the business mogul's $27bn empire, raising questions over whether she was excluded from the family trust, a court has been told.

There are so many topics to cover that it's hard to decide which order they should go in. We have started with the legal aspects, then gone on to tax considerations, and superannuation. After that, there's a range of topics that don't fall neatly under any of those categories. You can go straight to the area that you would like to understand first, but they do overlap. Let me say once again that the purpose of this book is to give you a basic understanding of the issues involved in effectively planning your estate. It is general advice only, and you should seek specific advice from an estate planning professional when you do your own estate planning.

When I was researching this part of the book, I asked the 37,000 people who subscribe to my newsletter to share their experiences with winding up estates and executorship. I have included some of the many replies I got. As you can imagine, numerous stories had the same themes: some reinforce the tips given throughout this book; and some show the amazing diversity of situations that can and do crop up.

Overwhelmingly, the takeaway from all the stories is twofold: "be prepared" and "expect the unexpected" when dealing with, and administering, death or loss of capacity in the family.

1

Your last will and testament

The cornerstone of estate planning is your will. This is how you provide for your loved ones after you pass away. A well-written and current will enables your estate to be settled quickly, without wasting time, effort, or money on legal fights.

In this chapter we'll begin to explain the things to be aware of when you make your will, who to talk to, how to ensure your will is valid, and how often you need to review it.

Someone will have to be the executor of your will, and this needs to be someone you trust, who is competent to do the work involved. We explain what they do, and how to help them enormously by giving them good information to start with.

We'll talk you through how and why wills are disputed, and help you understand how to head some problems off before they start. Let's get going.

Key terms	Explanation
Will / Testament	The legal document that sets out what someone wants to happen to their property after their death. "Testament" gives rise to the terms testator, testamentary (capacity/trust), and intestate, all of which are explained below.
Testator / Will-maker	The person who makes the will.
Intestate *(adj)* / Intestacy *(n)*	Dying without a will.
Testamentary capacity	The testator's ability, at the time of making the will, to understand what they were doing, and the nature and effect of their decisions.
Estate	The total of all assets you own at your death, from your clothes to your share portfolio.
Executor/s	The person or people nominated in a will to administer the estate of the deceased.
Administrator	Someone appointed by the court to administer a deceased person's estate if the person has died without a will, or their will is found to be invalid.
Legal personal representative (LPR) / Personal representative	A person who is legally authorised to represent a deceased individual and their estate. This term covers the executor/s or administrator of the estate.

Key terms	Explanation
Bequest *(n)* / Bequeath *(v)* / Disposition / Legacy	Any gift made by a will. This may range from Grandma's favourite tea service to a $3 million mansion.
Residue / Rest and residue	The balance of an estate after the distribution of specific gifts. For example, in an estate consisting of a house, car and jewellery, if you leave your house to your daughter, then the car and jewellery are the "rest and residue".
Beneficiary	Anyone named in a will to receive a benefit. This term is also used for people who benefit from a trust, in which context a beneficiary may have either a present or future interest.
Probate	The legal process of "proving" or validating your will after your death. Done by the Supreme Court in your state or territory.
Challenge (a will)	Mount a legal claim that a will is invalid.
Family provision application / Contest (a will)	An application to the courts for further or better provision from the estate for an eligible person. Eligibility rules vary, but generally include a spouse, child or dependant of the deceased person.

Function of a will

A valid will has many functions; the most important are:

1. Appointing someone responsible to administer your estate after your death.
2. Recording how you wish your assets to be distributed after your death.
3. Fulfilling your financial responsibilities after your death: discharging any debts and looking after any dependants.
4. Revoking or cancelling any old will/s.
5. Establishing a trust for your beneficiaries.

The whole idea of estate planning is to make sure that your assets end up in the hands of the people you think should receive them. A will appoints one or more executors of your estate, and then instructs them on how to distribute it.

So having a valid and up-to-date will is a major element of your estate planning. It is important to get your will prepared by a solicitor who is experienced in estate planning. It is a large and specialist area, and there are a lot of things to think about.

For example, a will can only deal with property that is in your name. Joint assets and assets held in a trust or owned by a company are not necessarily dealt with via the will. Superannuation is another type of asset that may not be dealt with in your will. It is important to discuss all these types of assets with the solicitor preparing your will.

Intestacy

If you don't have a will, or the will your survivors can locate is not valid, your estate will usually be distributed in terms of the law of intestacy. Contrary to popular opinion, the estates of intestate people do not automatically go to the government.

The provisions of intestacy laws vary from state to state, but essentially the rules are based on close family connections and next of kin, with the highest priority being given to the spouse (including de facto spouses) and children. Although the intent of the laws is good, their application often results in unintended and undesirable outcomes.

For example, assets may go to estranged family members, leaving out those you intended to inherit, or the government may take a portion of your estate if there are no surviving heirs. Imagine if you died without having made a will, and your spouse of 15 years was forced out of the family home because the administrator needed to sell it to share the proceeds with children from a previous marriage.

Another consideration of dying without a will is the enormous administrative headache you leave. Your family members will have to apply to the court for permission to administer your estate, and then locate all your assets. Even if your affairs are well organised, what you considered a simple filing system may be a complete mystery to the person trying to untangle your financial affairs.

CASE STUDY

My friend Harry, who lives in Australia, spent over 12 months rectifying the affairs of his brother, who died intestate. The brother, a 56-year-old divorcee, lived in New Zealand and was the ultimate procrastinator. He never got around to signing his will, and never got around to taking out travel insurance. The absence of travel insurance is of significance here — he died suddenly of a heart attack when he was travelling in Brazil.

It fell on Harry to arrange transport of his brother back to New Zealand, where his father was living in a nursing home, but there was one problem — bringing the body home would cost $30,000. Cremation would slash the transport costs but, under Brazilian law, cremation is prohibited unless the will specifically provides for it. As there was no will, Harry had to make a special application to the Brazilian authorities, through New Zealand solicitors, for permission to cremate his brother. This required a police report to be obtained from Brazil. As the report was in Portuguese, it had to be translated for the benefit of the lawyers in New Zealand. It took four months and $15,000 in fees to gain approval for the body to be cremated so the ashes could be sent home.

The brother's only asset was a $600,000 house. Under New Zealand intestacy laws, the entire estate of a single person goes to their parents, which means the entire estate was supposed to be paid to his father. He was in the early stages of dementia and was paying very low fees in a state-sponsored nursing home. A sudden bequest of $600,000 would render him ineligible for this type of accommodation and he certainly was not capable of dealing with the sum himself. But he had not given an enduring power of attorney to anybody to enable someone else to manage it for him.

Harry's next job was to apply to the New Zealand court for permission to administer the estate. This involved a New Zealand High Court barrister, an Australian lawyer, plus an additional lawyer for his father, to avoid any suggestion of conflict of interest. You can imagine the layers of fees incurred by all this.

Finally, after 12 months of frustration and expense, the matters were resolved and the proceeds split between Harry's father and the surviving siblings. Harry is well off himself and did not embark on the task of setting things right for the sake of the money — he was merely doing his duty as the eldest brother. However, as he points out, tens of thousands of dollars, and immeasurable angst, would have been saved if his brother had got around to signing his will.

A READER'S TALE

An accountant wrote: "I got a phone call from a woman — not a client — who told me her husband had died 10 days after coming back from cancer treatment overseas. There was no will, so his estate was with the Public Trustee. She had been trying to get a Centrelink pension, but it had been denied as she was apparently listed as a beneficiary in a trust controlled by her husband.

"She didn't know anything about a trust, or even who his accountant was. Centrelink gave her the ABN of the trust, but she said there is no way he would have that business name or location. She wanted me, as an accountant, to check his ATO Portal, but I can't legally do so, as she is not empowered to give me authorisation to do that.

"She said she's going to have to sell her home, as she has no income."

Capacity

Capacity refers to a person's ability to understand information, apply reasoning to that information, express a free and informed choice based on that information, and to understand the nature and consequences of their choices. Testamentary capacity is the ability to understand the nature and consequences of making a will, including how assets are to be distributed and any potential claims, and being of sound mind.

> *There is no possibility of mistaking midnight from noon, but at what precise moment twilight becomes darkness is hard to determine.*
>
> *Boyse v Rossborough (1857) HLC at 3.*

Capacity does not turn on and off like a light switch. It often declines gradually and, as the above quote eloquently states, it's hard to determine when this happens. Capacity can be affected temporarily by illness, medication, stress, trauma, grief, fatigue, and many other external factors. What's more, different types of decisions require different levels of capacity, e.g. someone may have the capacity to choose to enter into a new romantic relationship, but not the capacity to enter into a complex financial contract.

Testamentary capacity is important because if the will is challenged, for it to be upheld as valid, it must be able to be shown that the testator had testamentary capacity, knew and approved of the contents of the will, and that the will truly represents the testator's intention. The issue of capacity has given rise to much litigation and the courts have developed several well-established approaches to testing what needs to be established.

In *Timbury v Coffee (1941) 66 CLR 277, 283,* Dixon J wrote the matters necessary to establish testamentary capacity as follows:

> *Before a will can be upheld it must be shown that at the time of making it the testator had sufficient mental capacity to comprehend the nature of what he was doing, and its effects; that he was able to realise the extent and character of the property he was dealing with, and to weigh the claims which naturally ought to press upon him. In order that a man should rightly understand these various matters it is essential that his mind should be free to act in a natural, regular, and ordinary manner.*

We can summarise that as needing to:

- understand the nature and effect of the act of making a will
- understand the property to be disposed of by the will
- appreciate the claims (if any) that may be brought against the will, e.g. family provision claims
- be of sound mind.

To challenge the validity of a will based on lack of capacity, several elements must be demonstrated.

Firstly, it needs to be shown that the individual making the will did not possess the necessary capacity at the time of its creation. This could be due to factors such as dementia, mental illness, or being under the influence of alcohol, or recreational or prescription drugs.

Secondly, evidence must be provided to substantiate the claim of incapacity. This may include medical records, assessments from healthcare professionals, or witness testimonies from individuals who interacted with the person during the relevant period.

Moreover, it's essential to establish a causal link between the lack of capacity and the provisions within the will. This means demonstrating that the person's impaired mental state directly influenced the distribution of assets or beneficiaries outlined in the will.

To invalidate a will based on incapacity, the burden of proof rests on the party contesting its validity. They must present compelling evidence that convinces the court to set aside the will in question.

A good tip is, next time you review your will, also visit your GP and have a simple capacity assessment test done. Include that with your will. This serves as contemporaneous or "on the spot" evidence of your capacity at the time you made your will. This is particularly useful if you are thinking of dramatically changing your will to remove beneficiaries or reduce their gifts. Such a precaution could assist your executor to deflect any challenge to your testamentary capacity, and save your beneficiaries a great deal of trouble, stress, and expense.

Validity

For a will to be legally valid, a number of conditions must be satisfied.

- The intention of the will-maker must be unambiguous.
- The will-maker must have capacity to make a valid will — which means they must be mentally capable at the time of execution and understand the nature and effect of the document.
- They should be 18 years or over — if a person under 18 believes they need to make a will, they need to obtain court approval.
- The will-maker should be under no undue influence or pressure.

As outlined earlier, each state and territory has different legislation governing wills. These are known as the laws of succession, however there are some fundamental similarities.

- The will must be in writing.
- The will must be signed by the will-maker.
- The will-maker's signature must be witnessed as specified. Although the rules vary, this is always an important step to do properly. Typically, two witnesses are required, and you and your witnesses must all be present during the entire process of signing. The will-maker signs the will first, in the presence of the witnesses, and then each witness signs, and gives their full name, address and occupation where indicated.

  Your witnesses must:

  - be over 18 years of age and of "sound mind"
  - not be a beneficiary or (in some states) a spouse of a beneficiary: if they do witness your will, they are automatically disentitled from your will.

  It is also preferable that your witnesses:

  - are not your executors
  - use the same pen as the will-maker when signing the document. This is good evidence that all three people were together when the will was signed.

  The witnesses do not need to read the will — their sole function is to witness the will-maker physically sign the document.

As technology advances, there are now cases in the courts where unconventional wills have been found to be valid, because they expressed clear testamentary intention. For example, an unsent text message headed "My will", and a will recorded on a DVD have each been found by the court to be valid wills. However, these outcomes required lengthy and expensive court processes by the potential beneficiaries. Therefore, it is advisable to follow the conventions of traditional will-making.

For all the above reasons, it is best to have your will prepared and signed in a lawyer's office. It is always preferable that you see your solicitor alone. While you may have a family member or other trusted person sit in on the meeting, the solicitor must ask your consent and make sure that you are making that decision freely. Solicitors are aware of the risks of a person being unduly influenced by a family member when drafting a will.

As part of the will-making process, your lawyer will make notes, complete a questionnaire, and ask pertinent questions to clarify issues like soundness of mind and capacity. If you are over a certain age or are showing any sign that you do not understand some essential parts of the will-making process, the lawyer may suggest you obtain a capacity assessment from your doctor or a specialist.

Keeping your will

- Store your signed will in a safe place.
- Tell your executor/s where your will is kept, or give them a certified copy.
- Do not attach anything to it with a paper clip or staple. Any marks (including a mark from a rusty paper clip) must be explained to the court when probate is being sought after you pass away.
- Keep a list of your bank accounts, investments and any other details of your property with your will (but not attached to it). Update this frequently, as things change.
- Review your will every five years, or after something significant occurs, such as a marriage, divorce or death of a beneficiary or executor.

Preparing a will

Unless your affairs are very simple, there will be a wide range of factors to discuss with your solicitor and financial adviser when preparing your will.

There are three main types of wills, and three main approaches to preparing a will:

		Approach		
		Free	Cheap	Professional
TYPE	Simple	Y	Y	Y
	Testamentary Trust	N	N	Y
	Mutual	N	N	Y

We will also discuss one more type, the statutory will, which exists to cover more unusual situations and requires the input of the Supreme Court in your jurisdiction.

Although you can buy a do-it-yourself will kit from a newsagent, and it's common to see advertisements for cheap wills, or even free will preparation, these approaches are not recommended. The old adages "you get what you pay for" and "buy cheap, buy twice" apply — and in this case, if you get it wrong, it will be the beneficiaries of your estate who will suffer.

Inheritance laws are technical, and failure to comply with the technicalities could result in an invalid will. Furthermore, if superannuation is involved, or your beneficiaries have precarious financial circumstances or are in rocky relationships, or there are children from previous relationships, the will may be open to challenge or contest. This could mean a massive waste of both time and money for your survivors.

Remember, if you skimp on preparing your will, the dollar you save now may cost your beneficiaries dearly after your death. Since you are probably leaving your worldly resources to people you care about, do the right thing by them: get a competently drawn-up will, and update it as required to reflect changes in your circumstances.

It's wrong to think that you just need to make one will and that will is for life — that thinking belongs to an earlier era. You need expert advice to ensure your will reflects your wishes and then is updated regularly to take account of changing circumstances. This is particularly relevant to older people where aged care is involved, or if they take on a new relationship when their long-term partner dies.

Let me stress once more the cost and uncertainty of litigation if your will is disputed, not to mention the time and stress it may entail.

Types of wills

If you are calling a few solicitors to get an idea of their expertise and prices, one of their first questions is usually what type of will you need assistance with.

Simple wills

A simple will is one in which the will-maker is leaving their entire estate to their surviving partner or to their adult children in equal shares. It typically suits young or old people whose financial affairs and relationships are uncomplicated.

This is the only type of will that should ever be attempted on the cheap, or using a kit.

Testamentary trust wills

If your estate is substantial, a will that establishes a testamentary trust at your death might be useful. A testamentary trust passes your assets to a trustee to hold for the beneficiaries, rather than to the beneficiaries directly. It allows you to specify a particular way in which you wish the estate to be distributed, while still giving your beneficiaries some discretion about how and when to receive the funds. It can also be used to achieve flexibility in how it is distributed.

Having the assets held by a trust may be particularly helpful if the beneficiary is not good with money, is a bankrupt, or works in a profession that makes them likely to face a professional lawsuit, e.g. a doctor.

Make sure you obtain proper advice from both your solicitor and accountant to make sure the trust is of real advantage to your estate and your beneficiaries, and is not just a financial and administrative burden. Testamentary trusts incur ongoing administration costs to run the trust for as long as it is needed.

Mutual wills

Mutual wills are wills made by spouses or partners at the same time, with a contract to which they are both parties. This contract legally binds them not to change their respective wills without each other's consent. They are often used by couples who have children from previous relationships. They are typically created when both individuals want to make sure their respective assets are not subsumed into the surviving partner's estate.

If you are considering this type of will, get expert advice. That advice may often be simply, "Don't". I once asked a senior estate solicitor, "What do you know about mutual wills?" to which he responded, "I know enough to avoid them at all costs".

Once a mutual will is created and signed by both parties, it becomes a legally binding document that outlines how the assets of the couple will be distributed after their deaths. This may be reassuring for couples who want to ensure that their wishes are carried out after they pass away. But you are entering into a contract with your partner to neither revoke nor change your will. As life's circumstances change, you may want or need to break that promise, which can have expensive consequences for your estate.

There are some serious potential downsides to mutual wills. One is that mutual wills can be difficult to change once they are created. If one of the parties wants to make changes after the will has been signed, they may need to seek the other party's permission to do so, or risk breaching the contract to make mutual wills. In particular, this contract becomes final if one party to the contract loses testamentary capacity.

Also, leaving property by mutual wills does not remove the risk of the will being contested through a family provision application. Surviving spouses are still free to dispose of estate assets without breaching the contract for mutual wills, as long as any sale or disposal of assets is not an attempt to avoid a claim on the estate.

CASE STUDY

Years ago, John and Judy signed mutual wills leaving all their assets to each other, but with the proceeds to be split equally with their three young children if both parents died. Forty years have passed; John has dementia and lives in a nursing home, and their son — now aged 50 — has developed a serious addiction problem and is virtually bankrupt. The prudent strategy would be to change the will so that any money left to the problem child goes to a testamentary trust. Unfortunately, John has lost capacity and the mutual will must stand.

If John died first and Judy changed her will, while the second will would be admitted to probate, the provisions of the first will (as they related to the bankrupt son) would be held on trust for him. The court can enforce the contract arising from the mutual wills. By changing her will, Judy would also be breaching the contract between herself and John, which would make a claim for damages possible.

Statutory wills

What happens when a person is not capable of making a will? Where a person lacks testamentary capacity but it would be appropriate for them to have a will, it is possible to make an application to the Supreme Court in their state or territory for a statutory will. While each state and territory of Australia has their own legislation, the general concept is valid across the country. You would need to consult a qualified solicitor in your jurisdiction for detailed advice on your particular situation.

There are circumstances where some people have never had the necessary testamentary intent due to an impairment from birth or they have had capacity but have lost it due to impairment, illness or catastrophic injury.

Generally speaking, the court may make an order authorising a will to be made, altered or revoked on behalf of a person who is lacking in testamentary capacity. The order will only be made if the court is satisfied that the person lacks testamentary capacity and the proposed will is a reasonable representation of what the person would have wanted if they had capacity. This is also known as the "core test" and it differs from jurisdiction to jurisdiction.

For example, in South Australia, the proposed will has to "accurately reflect the likely intentions" of the person, but in Queensland the test is that the will "is or may be a will, alteration or revocation the relevant person would make if the person had testamentary capacity".

- The court must ensure that:
  - the person applying for the statutory will is an appropriate person (typically a spouse or partner, caregiver, legal guardian, or person with legal authority to act on behalf of the person, e.g. a solicitor)
  - adequate steps have been taken to ensure all interested parties were informed of the application.

A statutory will may be required:

- if the beneficiaries have predeceased the will-maker, leaving the will effectively void
- a draft will was made but not executed before the loss of testamentary capacity
- to avoid dying intestate, e.g. if there is a large estate and the person who has lost capacity never had a will

- to achieve asset protection despite the testator's loss of capacity, e.g. amending outright gifts to three sons to three testamentary trusts.

CASE STUDY

Paul suffers a catastrophic injury not long before he turns 18 years old, and receives a significant compensation payment. He is cared for by his elder brother. The family makes an application for a statutory will to ensure that his brother will be adequately provided for upon Paul's death. The court made an order for a statutory will to avoid him dying intestate.

Amending your will

There are two main ways to amend your will rather than creating a new one. To add detail, or explain why you have made the bequests you have, it is usually best to use a letter or memorandum of wishes. To make minor amendments to your will, a codicil (discussed on page 36) may be appropriate.

Letter (or memorandum) of wishes

A will is a legal document that is usually strictly drafted. It should not include extraneous information, such as messages to loved ones, or suggestions about what the testator may hope the beneficiary will do with any proceeds they receive from the estate. Such information can cause unnecessary complications and may lead to misunderstandings about the testator's intentions.

But a letter of wishes may be prepared at the same time as the will, or some time later, and it can be updated by the will-maker without fuss, and using their own words. It provides extra information for the executors, which was not included in the will itself, and is designed to be read in conjunction with the will. It may include instructions about funeral arrangements. It also enables the will-maker to express their preferences about how children will be raised in matters such as education, faith and culture. Some parents even include a lasting message for the beneficiaries, which may be of immense benefit to them when their parent dies.

A letter of wishes is often used to give personal possessions such as jewellery, paintings, or antique furniture to specific recipients. If appropriate, a spreadsheet or inventory could be annexed to the letter of wishes. It is much easier to keep this type of document updated than to do new wills.

A letter of wishes can also be used to explain the reasoning behind bequests. For example, if the bequests do not treat each beneficiary equally, the letter of wishes may explain why certain property is left to a particular child, and why — on the face of it — one child may have received an advantage over another. This is often relevant to rural families, where mum and dad have paid university fees for a few of the kids, while another one may have stayed back to run the farm, typically receiving a much lower income.

A letter of wishes can be useful to prevent costly court proceedings, as it helps the beneficiaries understand the reasoning for some of the decisions in the will. And if the will is challenged, a letter of wishes that conveys the thoughts of the testator to any potential challengers may enable a court to decide the issues quickly.

A solicitor friend tells me that describing reasons behind the gifting of assets may be better done by statutory declaration, because it is formally witnessed, which assists with challenges centring around duress and capacity. If your beneficiaries don't get along well, using a declaration rather than a letter is another way to protect them.

A letter of wishes can also be a useful document if the will-maker has young children. It may say how the deceased would like the children to be brought up, and may even include matters like a preferred religion, or a preferred school. The letter of wishes could also double as a letter from the will-maker to their children.

Keep in mind that this is not a legally binding document: it is guidance for the executor. It must be easy to locate, because it will be an essential tool for the executor when the estate is being wound up. Of course, nothing in a letter of wishes should contradict what is in the will.

I recommend preparing a letter of wishes in conjunction with the solicitor who prepares your will, at the same time as the will is being drawn up. If you do it on your own, without guidance, there is potential for it to conflict with the will and cause troubles down the track. Sadly, too many people say, "Oh, the children know who is to get what" — this has enormous potential to cause conflict.

A READER'S TALE

I believe that people need to be more careful about who they appoint as their executor and how their wills are enacted. It is insulting when family money is just thrown into the laps of those who did not earn it and may have played a game to make sure they took the hog's share of the estate.

I suggest individuals have a wish list specifying what they want done with items such as special photos or antiques, which may not be included in their wills.

Codicils

There may be times when you just want to make a minor adjustment to your will and don't want to go to the expense of getting an entirely new will drafted. An option that is commonly presented is a codicil. This is a Latin word — from the 15th century — and it literally means "short writing". However, codicils should be used with caution.

First, a codicil can be lost, as it is a separate document. Since it is made after the will, it is not referred to in your will, so it's possible that nobody would know to go looking for it, and any changes contained in the codicil would not be put into effect. Second, the codicil, unless very carefully drafted, can easily conflict with some terms of your will, making some clauses in your will void, or of no effect. Of course, codicils can be appropriate in some circumstances; however, it is important to discuss this with your solicitor and weigh up the pros and cons before adding a codicil to your will.

A READER'S TALE

A family friend, a very smart executive secretary, prepared her own will using a will kit. Over time she became very ill and died, leaving problems for her executor. The executor did nothing, so after a year I suggested a solicitor be appointed to deal with the problem and I would pay the cost. This was done and probate proceeded.

She wanted to leave substantial sums of money to three parties, and this money was to be paid from a life insurance policy. All other assets went to her husband. Unfortunately, the policy was not to be paid to the estate to be dealt with by the executor according to the will — the insurer held instructions to pay proportions direct to the beneficiaries after probate was granted. The proportions did not agree with those in the will, and the insurer could only go with the instructions they held.

Eventually I sorted it out by agreement with the parties to be in line with the will. An incredibly simple estate had been made difficult by a smart person drafting a will with simple — but expensive and time-consuming — errors. My advice is to always employ a professional, no matter how simple the estate. The appointment of the solicitor to resolve this clash cost several times the cost of a will, even before you figure in the costs of the delay and extra work.

Parties to a will

There are two main parties involved when a will is executed: the executor/s and the beneficiaries.

The will must appoint an executor, who can also be a beneficiary. The role of the executor is to distribute the assets to the beneficiaries in accordance with the will. We'll look at that in detail now.

Executors

As mentioned earlier, depending on the type of will, an executor can also be known as a legal personal representative, administrator or even trustee. There can also be multiple executors. For simplicity, we will refer to a single executor in this book, except when explaining issues relevant to multiple executors.

An executor has numerous powers, including the power to sell property, invest, carry on a business or litigate on behalf of the estate. Therefore it is important to carefully choose your executor, and you may even like to suggest that they engage a lawyer to assist them with the administration. The executor can also be personally liable for their conduct and management of the estate.

Each state and territory has slightly different laws in relation to administration of an estate. However, they all include time limits that apply for potential beneficiaries to make a claim on the estate. Your executor must not distribute the estate until these time limits have passed.

An estate solicitor tells me: "Acting as an executor has the potential to be a very stressful and onerous task. I always advise clients to speak to their intended executor and seek their consent to act. It can put them in an undesirable situation, especially if they are the uncle/aunt to the children.

"Sometimes, in their capacity as executor, decisions have to be made which will be considered by one child as favouring one over another. A major and common decision is whether the family home should be kept or sold.

"I also caution against appointing only one child as executor, as that too is fraught with danger."

Executor responsibilities and duties

To help you choose an appropriate executor, it is helpful to understand what you are asking them to do. Your executor is responsible for:

- the administration of your estate
- paying debts and taxes
- distributing assets to your beneficiaries according to the terms of your will.

This may be a fairly easy job if the estate is a simple one, but if it's complex with investments and properties, some big decisions may need to be made. In this case, it may be fertile ground for conflict, especially if the beneficiaries don't get on, or if they have different business experience.

READER TIPS: WHAT I WISH I'D KNOWN AT THE START

I have just completed the wind-up of my mother's estate. It looked pretty simple on paper, as it was just cash at bank and refundable accommodation deposit (RAD) from a nursing home group.

What I learned:

- Get a death certificate as soon as possible and have at least four copies certified.
- Grant of probate is needed for estates over $50,000, as a rule of thumb.
- When the grant of probate comes through, get it certified by a JP or a solicitor. Again, at least four copies.

I had to deal with Tricare for the RAD. They would not accept sighting of the physical certificate or even a certified copy that I was prepared to deliver to their head office to release the RAD. It had to be a direct email from my solicitor to their finance people. Go figure. Some other providers may have different rules. I asked for the $375,000 RAD, plus interest, to be made out to me as the executor, for disbursement to me and my siblings. They refused. They do not do bank cheques. In the end, they insisted I open an account at Mum's bank in the name of "The Estate of the Late ….." Then they finally paid the money into the bank account.

Mum's bank (NAB) proved to be very difficult and inefficient to deal with. They have a so-called 'bereavement team', which is a call centre in Melbourne head office, and some of them have poor English. I won't go into all the issues I had, but lost or misplaced documents, multiple contacts with staff who would only give first names, lack of return of phone calls, lack of response to emails, and 45 minutes 'on hold' in five phone calls, only begins to describe the issues. It was the most frustrating thing I have had to do in a long time. In the end, I penned an email to the CEO of NAB, and within two hours the manager of the bereavement team rang, full of apologies, and the whole thing got sorted out in hours.

The estate is now wound up. On reflection, I hate to think how an executor with limited knowledge of the corporate world, limited knowledge of technology, and ordinary communication skills would cope.

Administration

The duties of the executor would normally include:

- obtaining a death certificate (this typically takes about six weeks to issue, and it may be needed for many of the following tasks) and at least five certified copies
- locating the current will
- preparing an inventory of the estate's assets and liabilities
- notifying the beneficiaries
- applying for, and obtaining, a grant of probate
- opening an estate bank account: "The estate of the late …"
- consolidating assets of the estate into the estate bank account, i.e. closing other bank accounts and transferring funds, superannuation (if applicable), and proceeds of sale of property, etc.
- liaising with an accountant to find out if a tax return needs to be prepared for the deceased and a tax return lodged for the estate
- notifying the relevant authorities
  - Australian Taxation Office
  - Australian Electoral Commission
  - Centrelink, including applying for bereavement allowance, if appropriate. (If you receive an income

support payment you may be eligible for this payment for up to 14 weeks after the death of your partner, instead of your usual payment, subject to an income and assets test.)

- notifying the following parties so that services can be finalised and final accounts paid:
  - utilities, including electricity, gas, mobile telephone, landline telephone and internet
  - any subscriptions, e.g. journals, streaming services
  - private health insurers and Medicare
  - any groups of which the deceased was a member
- cancelling their driver licence
- redirecting mail
- notifying car, house, and contents insurers and finding out what arrangements need to be made in regard to insurance cover
- changing any automatic deductions from the deceased's bank account.

As the executor consolidates the estate assets, each bank, superannuation fund and investment organisation will require the executor to satisfy their respective verification of identity (VOI) processes. So the executor needs multiple certified copies of their personal identification documents, in addition to the death certificate and grant of probate.

READER TIP: CHECK AND SEARCH

You will need lots and lots of documents to be certified at multiple stages of the process. In the ACT there is a Justice of the Peace rostered on at each police station and they don't charge for their services. It could end up costing you a lot if you were paying someone by the page.

Paperwork is becoming increasingly complicated. I recently had to try to establish the cost base of shares bought between 1975 and now. There are online records for share prices from 2000, but I found it hard to find records before that.

Also, you may have to go through a lot of possessions and paperwork in a short time if you are cleaning out a house. Check, check, and check again before you dispose of any paperwork. I got my piles mixed up and ended up throwing away some things I should have kept for capital gains tax purposes. There was no way of getting those back. It wasn't the end of the world, but had I kept them, Mum would have saved a few thousand dollars in tax.

And if you are cleaning out a dwelling, check everything for stashes. My grandmother had quite a bit of cash hidden in various places. We made a bit of a game of it, with the whole family going through everything and putting the money in a box in the lounge room. I was amazed to find that it totalled in the thousands. She had been through the wars and had learnt to save. It was pretty good going for someone on the pension. (Perhaps you could call it "personally valuable items").

A READER'S TALE

We cancelled my father's internet account soon after he moved into care, as my mother sold their apartment to fund his RAD and move closer to me, her only child. She did not use the internet or emails. We didn't realise that closing his account would deny access to my father's emails. There may have been emails that required attention, but we had to hope such a sender would get in contact by other means, such as mail. Fortunately we had the password to my father's computer — it would have been very difficult without it. We backed up all his files onto my computer and many of these files have come in handy in the years since. My parents had joint bank accounts, and when the bank was later advised of my father's death, access was denied for a week or so. I recommend withdrawing sufficient funds before advising the bank.

Estate management

The executor is legally responsible for the management of the assets of the estate. It is important, if there is a property, that the insurance is kept up to date and the property is maintained before sale. A disgruntled beneficiary could make life difficult for an executor who has failed in their duties and diminished the value of the estate.

It is important to account for any funds an executor personally spends, and which require reimbursement by the estate. This means you must keep any invoices/receipts so that you can show the beneficiaries where the funds have been spent when it is time to disburse the funds from the estate bank account.

Estate management can be a complex and time-consuming job. If the estate is complicated, expert legal advice should be taken before major decisions are made. However, if the estate is a fairly simple one, a couple often appoint the survivor of the deceased partner as executor. If the surviving spouse is unable or unwilling to act, the role may then pass to adult children, who may be appointed to act jointly or individually. This is not a simple issue, and you will need to discuss the best options with your legal advisers.

A READER'S TALE

I was 84 when my husband died. Almost everything we owned was in joint names, with the exception of a few shares that were in his name only. For the most part it was just a case of presenting the death certificate and having things changed into just my name. We had always shared responsibility for financial matters, so I knew what had to be done and how to do it. One place I struck a problem was at the Department of Transport, where the lass I dealt with did not know that because our vehicle was in joint names it automatically went to me. However, she stuck with it until she found the relevant information. Everything was made much easier because I knew all the details of our finances.

Years ago we went on a long caravan trip and I typed up a document with all our financial details, banks, pensions, insurance, shareholdings, etc, which we gave to our children, along with an enduring power of attorney, in case anything happened to us on our trip. I keep that document updated and periodically send them an updated copy. The document also tells them where to find important files, such as shareholdings, birth certificates, and marriage certificates, in my filing cabinets and where to find any files on my computer that they might need: basically everything they will need to know when I am gone is in that document. Separately, and on paper, to avoid having a record on my computer or phone, I have given them the passwords for my computer and password file and the code for my phone. I guess I am fortunate in that I have complete trust in my children not to abuse the information I have given them.

Paying debts and taxes

Your estate remains liable for all your debts and ongoing expenses. Once you pass away, however, all of your accounts will be frozen. Banks generally will release funds for the payment of the funeral only after presentation of an invoice. But your death does not stop bills such as rates, utilities, insurance and taxes arriving, and they must be paid. This means that executors are often called on to pay the bills on your behalf, and may be left several thousand dollars out of pocket for months before they can be reimbursed.

A READER'S TALE

My elderly father passed away a couple of years ago. My mother predeceased him, and he sold the family home when he moved into aged care at age 90. He had no other assets, so the net proceeds of the sale of his home (less the substantial aged care accommodation bond) was sitting in his bank account. He was not interested in investing this money and enjoyed knowing that he had more than $1 million in the bank. My sister and I paid all of his ongoing costs from his bank account, so there was a high level of financial transparency for everyone.

When he passed away, my sister and I (both executors and the primary beneficiaries of the estate) had to advise the bank, which then froze his account. However, I was advised by our solicitor to withdraw sufficient funds from his account, prior to notifying the bank, to cover foreseeable expenses — such as funeral costs and legal disbursements, including probate filing costs. I opened a new account and transferred $14,000 of my father's money into it to pay these costs. If I had not done so, I would have had to pay these costs from my own savings (as my sister would not have been able to contribute) and waited nine months or so for probate to be granted and the estate to be distributed before I could be repaid.

A good tip (if you can afford it) is to open a joint bank account with the executor and deposit sufficient funds to pay your bills for six months. As it is a joint account, when you pass away, the account is still accessible by the other account holder. Of course, you need to make sure your executor can access the account, and also reconsider this if you change executors.

Distributing assets

Distribution can only be made when the executor is certain that all debts of the deceased and their estate have been paid and there are no claims on the estate from either creditors or family members.

A READER'S TALE

My great-aunt died without a will. She had never married, lived alone and was a hoarder. She was also extremely wealthy after a lifetime of wise investments. She had one brother and two sisters; all three siblings were on the pension.

Her brother was appointed by the court as administrator and proceeded to travel with his elderly sisters five hours to the house where my great-aunt lived, to try to get the house in order. The house was full of 40 years of collecting all manner of random items.

The siblings spent their collective savings of almost $20,000 on skip bins, garden clearing, tree lopping, pest management and attending to broken windows and locks. Once some of the assets started to be deposited into the estate bank account they approached the solicitor administering the estate to be reimbursed, only to be told they were not entitled to reimbursement or an early bequest until all of the assets were collected and debts paid. They had to wait 11 months to get anything at all from the estate. They had had no idea they would have to wait so long, and it put them under considerable financial stress.

A READER'S TALE

My brother passed away after being diagnosed with an aggressive form of cancer. Once diagnosed, he was told he should ensure all matters were "sorted out" urgently, as it was expected he would only live for a month or two.

My brother had no will, no children, no partner, no solicitor, and no financial adviser. He agreed for a solicitor to visit him in hospital to prepare a will, and I was appointed executor. His will was straightforward, with beneficiaries being several charities, and his niece and nephew.

He withdrew most of the money from his super to avoid the death tax. We closed all bank accounts except one. I even had time to help him complete his 2022 tax return. After he died, probate was finalised, his house was sold and proceeds deposited to the solicitor's trust account for distribution to the beneficiaries.

Then the Commonwealth Bank wrote detailing fees of $30,000 he had been charged for services he never received. Without consultation, CBA sent the funds to BT Australia, as he had once had a superannuation account there. BT no longer had an account for him and remitted the funds to the ATO.

These funds are still to be returned to my brother's estate, and this matter has proved to be a major battle with the ATO.

MyGov and the ATO have been nothing but a severe pain. Once advised of my brother's death, all access to his accounts has been closed. As his executor, I applied for access to his ATO account in March 2023, and for the return of the funds forwarded to them in November 2022 by BT Australia.

When I contacted the ATO enquiring about my applications, I was advised that, as 28 days had passed, they would be reviewed and processed shortly. Since then, I have called each month and have been consistently advised that they are understaffed, have a huge backlog, and can give no indication as to when these applications will be reviewed.

I am left grieving, angry, and unable to finalise his estate or distribute funds to his beneficiaries.

READER TIP: PREVENT THEFT

All property should be protected (locked up) to stop looters — especially relatives who just walk in and clean out whole areas without permission. The sheds on my uncle's property were cleaned out by his brother-in-law of very expensive heavy machinery, and no one did a thing about it.

Choosing your executor/s

The choice of an executor is an important decision that requires careful consideration. You should choose someone who is trustworthy, organised, competent, available, has a good relationship with your beneficiaries, and — if possible — is younger and healthier than you. They will need to administer your estate efficiently, seek appropriate advice, and finalise your estate in an appropriate timeframe. An ineffective executor can make life difficult for your beneficiaries when they are already grieving your passing, delay distribution, and be the subject of complaints or court action. By selecting the right executor, you can help to ensure that your estate is managed correctly and your wishes are carried out after your death.

So, let's look at what makes a good executor in more detail:

- **Trustworthiness:** You want someone honest, who can be relied on to act in the best interest of your beneficiaries; someone who has demonstrated integrity and responsibility in their personal and professional life. Appointing more than one executor, especially if they are appointed jointly, means that your executor knows someone else is seeing what they do, which tends to keep people from temptation, but can introduce other complications.

- **Organisational skills:** The executor should be able to keep track of important documents, deadlines, and financial records. They should be able to manage the estate efficiently and effectively, ensuring that all the necessary paperwork is filed on time and that your beneficiaries receive their inheritance promptly.

You can also include a direction in your will for your executor to use the services of a lawyer to assist with estate administration. If this is the case, ensure that the will specifies the law firm by name, rather than the individual solicitor, who may leave the firm or predecease you.

- **Competence:** Choose someone who is capable and confident in their ability to either work with lawyers, accountants, and financial advisers to ensure that your estate is managed correctly or navigate the process themselves.
- **Availability:** The executor should be available to manage your estate promptly after your death. They should be willing and able to take on this responsibility and have the time and energy to devote to it. This is a hard one to predict, since you don't know when you will die.
- **Relationship with beneficiaries:** The executor should have a good relationship with your beneficiaries and be able to communicate with them effectively. This can help to avoid conflicts and ensure that your wishes are carried out.
- **Age and health:** It's important to choose an executor who is likely to outlive you and is in good health.

How many executors?

It is always good practice to appoint at least two executors. Some claim that it is best to appoint them 'jointly', which means they both have to agree on all actions taken, but this can cause all sorts of complications, so appointing one executor, with a backup to be executor if the first is unable or unwilling to act, is another excellent option.

If you are appointing more than one executor you should have confidence that they are compatible and will be able to work together. Also, put some thought into where your executor/s live. It is much harder to execute an estate from overseas, and hardest of all with joint executors in different locations, as they will both have to sign documents.

Older couples often appoint their spouse as executor but also add a child, so there will be a backup if the first executor is unable to act. Some people might even consider appointing all the children, to prevent family fights, but that is not always a good solution.

In cases where executors find it impossible to cooperate and agree on how to manage the estate's administration, they may seek legal assistance to resolve the matter. If one or both executors mutually decide to terminate their roles, they must make an application to the Supreme Court to be removed from their positions. The court may then appoint an administrator to replace them.

Ideally, executors would consider the estate's best interests and ensure that the administration continues smoothly despite their conflict. If the will specifies that both executors must agree on decisions, and they can't come to an agreement, the court's intervention may be necessary to prevent a deadlock.

A READER'S TALE

My mother has died, and Dad's will leaves my sister and me as joint executors. After helping Dad handle Mum's estate, I now know how much work could be involved in finalising Dad's estate — property, assets, and all the little things, and I have started to have nightmares about how that would ever get done with my sister.

Neither of us really trust each other, and she and her new partner seldom agree with anything I say. She also lives interstate and is very slack at answering correspondence. Another issue is how we would decide which jobs would fall to each person. I think there's a time limit on finalising an estate so you can't argue about arrangements indefinitely. I guess you could take the other person to court about it — more stress!

A READER'S TALE

I was one of four executors for my mother's estate, and we were appointed as joint executors. Because we all lived in different cities, when documents were to be signed, we had to use snail mail to each person in a round-robin arrangement to sign off each form as required. This was a real time-waster. One executor appointed at a time is more than sufficient. I suggest people appoint one main executor, with a couple for backup. Also, the executor's permission should be obtained before the will is made.

Appointing a solicitor as executor

There is the option to appoint a solicitor as the executor of your will, but this is not usually the preferred option unless the will-maker has no close friends or family, and wants the estate to be used for philanthropic purposes. Other situations when a solicitor may be a suitable choice include when the will-maker:

- lives in Australia, but their only child is resident in an overseas country
- has no surviving family and wishes to leave money to various friends and acquaintances
- foresees family disharmony arising after their death — a professional, non-family executor may be a wise choice in these circumstances.

Bear in mind that not all solicitors are willing to take on this role, and they are not obligated to do so. Our suggestion is to consider appointing a solicitor as executor only when there are no practical alternatives, keeping in mind that a solicitor would charge your estate for this service. You would have to ensure that there is an appropriate charging clause in your will, which gives permission for the solicitor to charge for their services. Fees are normally at an hourly rate. Some groups charge a percentage of the estate instead, but in my view, an hourly rate is a much fairer method of payment. Make sure you are comfortable with whatever is proposed.

Deciding whether to appoint a solicitor from your local area or elsewhere is largely a personal decision. Most solicitors willing to be executors are competent in fulfilling this duty. It's essential to communicate directly with your chosen solicitor to confirm their willingness and ensure you are comfortable with your decision. Considering the unpredictability of life, it's advisable to nominate the name of the legal firm rather than the name of the solicitor. This will cover circumstances such as the solicitor leaving that practice or predeceasing you.

Appointing a trustee company as executor

If it's not possible to find an appropriate executor, you could consider a trustee company whose sole role is to administer estates. These are usually large institutions. The advantages are that they have eternal life and should be well experienced in the role of an executor. However, most of them charge a percentage of the estate, so if the estate is a big one their fee could be quite large. I have heard complaints that some trustee companies are rather bureaucratic and are never in a rush to get the job done. It's really a matter of making up your own mind. Maybe it's possible to speak to friends you know who have had dealings with them.

Accepting an appointment as executor

If a family member, friend, or colleague asks to appoint you as executor, think carefully before you accept. To help you decide, get them to talk you through the items that comprise the estate. The following case study gives you a hint of the possible ramifications of taking on the role without really understanding what it will involve. This was an extreme situation, but it does highlight the challenges that could arise for anyone taking on the role of executor without sufficient knowledge of the job they will have to do.

CASE STUDY

Sue was single, aged 55, and had an administrative role with a bank. She was on good terms with her neighbour Hank, who had migrated to Australia 20 years ago with his wife. She had died a few years earlier and he was still a widower. Hank always regarded Sue as an honest and capable person and when he was re-doing his will, he asked her if she was prepared to be the executor. Sue was the kind of person who is always keen to help out, and she agreed to act for him. Three years later, she woke to find an ambulance outside Hank's house — the paramedics told her that he had just passed away.

Immediately her mind was full of questions: What funeral director should she use? Was Hank to be cremated or buried? How could she contact his next of kin and friends to advise of his death? Where was his will?

Luckily, she had a key to his house, so she went inside and rummaged through some cupboards. She did find an original will, and some insurance papers, but she also discovered rates notices and land tax notices for a commercial building in Sydney. To further complicate matters, she found details of investments in both direct shares and property syndicates in his filing cabinet. The will provided for part of his estate to be given to charity, but much of the estate was left to relatives who lived overseas.

Her normally simple life was suddenly in turmoil. Sue had to plan his funeral, arrange for the sale of his house, and decide what to do with his rental property and other investments. With no local family, she also had to answer mundane questions like who will clean out his cupboards and the refrigerator. She was also faced with a possible sale of the commercial property, as well as contacting the overseas beneficiaries.

A final consideration before you accept a role as executor is that initially it can be very costly — once someone passes away, all of their accounts will be frozen. Executors often end up paying the deceased person's bills for months before they can be reimbursed. Banks generally will release funds for the funeral, but only after presentation of the invoice. Only joint accounts remain accessible, which is why it is helpful to set one up with your executor, as explained on page 48, and to transfer money to it before you die.

A READER'S TALE

My father died in 2021 and my sister, my brother and I were listed as executors.

The three of us had to open up accounts with his bank — Great Southern — in the name of the estate. They required original signatures from the three of us. My sister lives in the UK, my brother on the north coast, and I live in Sydney. So I would email the form to my sister, who would fill in her section and sign it. She would snail mail it to my brother for him to complete and sign. He would snail mail it to me. I would then complete the form, sign it and mail it to GSB. The process took weeks. This business of companies requiring original paper documents from the three of us was a continuing theme.

As an executor, your job is to gather together all the assets of the estate. The three of us decided the best course of action was to convert everything to cash then divide into three (which was what my father's will stated). This involved selling shares, but the two major share registries (Computershare and Link Market Services) required different paperwork.

When it came to distributing the cash (just under $1 million) we ran into more problems, because online transfers were limited to $30,000. This could be increased to $100,000 if the three executors agreed, but the increase was only valid for 24 hours, and it had to be done via message in the GSB app. I would phone GSB at 8 AM to request the increase. My brother and sister would then each have to open their app to approve the request when it came through. This was always after midnight for my sister in the UK.

These processes made the work of administering the estate much harder than it needed to be.

What happens if an executor becomes unable or unwilling to act?

Executors can renounce their role in writing by making an application to the Supreme Court before they begin acting, if they wish to be relieved of their responsibilities.

If they begin to administer the estate but then become unable or unwilling to perform their duties, Australian law provides two options to ensure the administration of the deceased's estate proceeds smoothly. These options apply whether the executor has died, lost capacity, is unwell, or is simply too busy with a more pressing matter to take on the extra work.

1. If more than one person was appointed, the remaining executor/s can continue the administration.
2. If only one executor was appointed, or all appointed executors are unable or unwilling to act, someone must apply to the supreme court to be appointed administrator. There is an established priority of persons (close relatives, beneficiaries, attorneys or public trustees, or creditors) who may apply, and the court's decision will be based on the best interests of the estate and the beneficiaries. The administrator becomes responsible for distributing the assets according to the will, or in accordance with intestacy laws if there is no will.

Beneficiaries

Anyone to whom you leave anything in your will is a beneficiary: they benefit from your will. If you have dependants and you do not provide for them in your will, you can expect them to contest the will, and that mostly benefits the lawyers, so your will is not the best place to have a tantrum. Other than that, you may leave vastly different types of bequests. Choosing appropriate beneficiaries can be a complex matter, and even when leaving assets to your children, it's not always a matter of simply dividing the money between them equally.

There are many issues to consider, and what follows are merely suggestions — not a comprehensive list — to get you thinking, so you can have a meaningful conversation with your solicitor, financial adviser, and accountant when drawing up your will. Many of these issues are discussed in greater depth in later chapters.

Predictable financial considerations for beneficiaries

Unless the estate consists only of cash in the bank, you need to understand that not all assets are treated equally for tax purposes, which means that leaving equal amounts in different forms may result in completely different amounts being received by each person — and that's before applying their own differing tax rates.

For example, the family home is normally exempt from capital gains tax, as are assets that were bought before

20 September 1985 when capital gains tax (CGT) was introduced. I'll discuss CGT in detail later, but for now keep in mind that death does not automatically trigger CGT — it merely passes the liability to the beneficiaries, who will pay CGT if and when they dispose of the asset left to them. This is a particularly important issue if the beneficiary is a non-resident of Australia for tax purposes.

If a potential beneficiary has their own business, it's important to think about the financial stability of that business. You don't want money you leave to a beneficiary ending up in the hands of creditors if the business goes bust.

You should also consider the potential effects of any bequests on any government payments, such as the age pension. I regularly get emails from people who are on the full pension, have received an unwanted bequest and don't know what to do with it.

If the will-maker is under 60, the tax effect of any superannuation proceeds that may come from a life insurance policy held in super needs to be considered.

Treating your children equally

Most people want to treat their children "equally", but thanks to the vicissitudes of life they may have special needs as time goes by. Maybe there is inequality between the income of the beneficiaries, possibly they've been given money for education or a home deposit, maybe they have suffered a financial emergency, and you've been the one to bail them out. The crunch comes when you are deciding what to put in your will. You will need to discuss with your solicitor if special arrangements need to be made to even things up, if some of your children have benefited in advance. A friend who specialises in mediation for deceased estates tells me that the more transparent the process of deciding on and implementing any differences, the less likely it is that there will be problems.

People also have quite different attitudes to, and experience in, handling money. One of your potential beneficiaries may be a smart money manager; another may be a spendthrift. If you want both beneficiaries to benefit from your hard-earned money, it may be useful to insert some kind of trust in the will for the beneficiary who needs it.

If one of the beneficiaries is young, you may believe that they should not receive a substantial sum until they are mature enough to handle it. Or a person may have a mental or physical disability that means they will never be able to handle the money on their own. In such cases, the will may include a testamentary trust, of which they are a beneficiary. The bequest goes to a trust, not the person themselves; then it is the trustee who is responsible for handling the money. More on this later.

If a person is in a relationship that breaks down, the other party may be entitled to a share of that person's assets. There are no hard and fast rules, because each case depends on individual circumstances. However, if you have any reason to think the relationship may not be permanent, take advice about the best way to handle that bequest.

You may also choose to exclude some people who expect to be beneficiaries — for a range of reasons. If this is the wish of the will-maker, the solicitor will need to take great care in drafting the will to reduce the chance of challenges and contests to the estate.

Beneficiary options if an executor seems incompetent or dishonest

If beneficiaries believe the appointed executor is incompetent or not fulfilling their obligations properly, they may take legal action to address their concerns. Beneficiaries have the right to apply to the court to have an executor removed or replaced if they can provide sufficient evidence of incompetence, negligence, or misconduct. Remember, executors have a legal obligation to act diligently and in the best interests of the estate. The court will carefully assess the situation and make a decision based on the best interests of the estate and the beneficiaries.

Seek legal advice before pursuing such actions, as the process can be complex and requires proper documentation and evidence to substantiate the claims against the executor.

Disputing a will

Two terms are often used together when it comes to disputing a will, but their meanings are quite different, as are their outcomes. In brief:

- **to challenge a will** means to allege that it was invalid. Anyone can challenge a will and, if successful, the entire will may be declared null and void.
- **to contest a will** means to claim it is not fair. Only an eligible person may contest a will, by claiming they have not received what they feel is a proper provision as a dependant or family member. As a result, the distribution of the original will may be altered.

Challenging the validity of a will

Challenges to wills on the grounds of lack of capacity, undue influence, fraud, mistake, duress or lack of testamentary intention are not limited to specific categories of people. A challenge to a will on those grounds can be brought, for example, by a person or persons who had an entitlement under a prior valid will but have been excluded from the second will in suspicious circumstances. Such a challenge could invalidate a word, a clause or an entire will.

Grounds for challenging a will

Challenging a will involves proving that there are legitimate grounds for challenging its validity or fairness. These include:

- **Lack of testamentary capacity:** The deceased was not of sound mind when they created the will, and lacked the mental capacity to understand the implications of their decisions.
- **Undue influence:** The deceased was pressured, manipulated, or unduly influenced by another person when making decisions about their will. This could involve situations where a caregiver or family member exercises inappropriate control over the deceased's decisions.
- **Fraud or forgery:** The authenticity of the will is in doubt, e.g. it may have been forged, or created under false pretences.

The process of challenging a will

Challenging a will is not a decision to be taken lightly. It involves navigating legal intricacies — and costs — while grappling with intense emotions surrounding the loss of a loved one. This is why it's so important for anybody considering challenging a will to seek professional advice, to ensure they fully understand the process and the potential outcomes.

Challenging a will involves several steps:

1. **Legal advice:** Challengers should seek legal advice from experienced estate lawyers. A lawyer will determine the contestant's eligibility, assess the case's merits, guide the contestant on the appropriate grounds, and explain the legal process.

2. **Application:** File an application in the appropriate court challenging the validity of the will.

3. **Court proceedings:** The executor initially has to prove to the court that the will is valid and then the responsibility shifts to the person disputing the validity of the will. The solicitor who drafted the will is also required to give evidence on circumstances of the execution of the will.

4. **Outcome and costs:** The court will issue a decision outlining whether the claim is successful and what adjustments, if any, need to be made to the will; a word, clause or entire will can be declared invalid. It's important to note that the losing party may be liable for legal costs.

Contesting the provisions of a will

The rules for contesting a will, and who is eligible to do so, are slightly different in each state, but in essence, they aim to include the deceased person's spouse, children and/or any person who is financially dependent on the will-maker.

While family provision claims might seem daunting, and the question of the purpose of making a will arises, understanding their implications is crucial to a satisfactory outcome.

There's usually a deadline for making a claim, and while it may be possible to obtain an extension of time, the court will consider matters such as the reason for the delay, the behaviour of those involved, and the strength of the application. Extensions are often refused if the estate has already been distributed, and estates should generally be finalised within 12 months of the date of death.

Bear in mind that not every will can be successfully contested. A well-considered and thoughtfully drafted will can significantly reduce the likelihood of a claim — or negate the need for one altogether. But no matter how well the will is drafted, it is not possible to avoid a family provision claim. If an applicant is eligible, and can demonstrate they have been left without proper provision, they may make a claim.

What is an appropriate amount in a particular case is largely based on an individual's perceptions. It is not a case where mathematical certainty can be applied. There are longstanding principles that a spouse should be left with secure accommodation and enough income to support themselves. But this can become complex where there are second marriages, particularly if children of the first marriage expect to inherit what was their family home. In an attempt to avoid any contest, some testators include a right to reside or a life tenancy for the second spouse, but such matters should be carefully considered and legal advice obtained.

It is not possible to include a gift in the will that is conditional on the beneficiary not making a claim on the estate.

In circumstances where there is a will and a financial agreement pursuant to the *Family Law Act 1975 (Cth)* it is essential that the solicitor drafts both documents together, to ensure that one does not contradict the other and give rise to a family provision application.

Grounds for contesting a will

A claim for "further and better provision" may be brought by an eligible person who has been left out of the will or believes the bequest they received was insufficient for their needs. Anybody thinking of contesting a will will need legal advice to determine their eligibility.

The categories of people entitled to make a claim for further and better provision vary from state to state. They include spouses, including de facto spouses; children, including stepchildren in some states; and financial dependants. Generally speaking, former spouses have no claim on the estate, particularly if a property settlement has been finalised. If the former spouse is still financially dependent on the deceased, then there could be limited circumstances where they could make a claim.

Family provision claims must be substantiated with evidence supporting the claimant's reasons for seeking provision. Claims that include vague demands for expensive accommodation, or specific types of housing without adequate justification, may face hurdles in court.

There is a common misconception that legal costs will be borne by the estate, but this isn't always the case. If the court refuses the application for further and better provision — particularly if the estate is small — it's also likely that any request for costs to come out of the estate will be refused. As with most legal actions, an inherent risk in family provision claims is the possibility of an adverse costs order. Unsuccessful claimants may find themselves obligated to pay costs.

Testators hold the freedom to determine the fate of their estates, so the court intervenes only when it becomes evident that the deceased failed to make adequate provision for the claimant. The court's role is to find a compromise between the will-maker's wishes and the legitimate claims of potential beneficiaries. It seeks a balance between testamentary freedom and the responsibilities of the will-maker.

The process of contesting a will

Contesting a will involves several steps:

1. **Legal advice:** An experienced estate lawyer will determine the contestant's eligibility, assess the case's merits, guide the contestant on the appropriate grounds, and explain the legal process. The first thing to establish is whether you have been left without adequate provision from the estate for your maintenance and support. If this is the case, then the second step is what provision, if any, should be made from the estate.

2. **Application:** An application must be filed in the appropriate court seeking further and better provision from the deceased for your maintenance and support.

3. **Court proceedings:** To determine whether adequate provision has been made from the estate for the contestant's maintenance and support, the court will consider, among other things: the applicant's financial position; the size and nature of the deceased's estate; the whole relationship between the applicant and the deceased; and the relationship between the deceased and other people who have legitimate claims upon the estate.

4. **Outcome and costs:** The court will determine whether the claim is successful and what the applicant is entitled to. A word, clause or entire will can be altered to make further provision for the applicant. If the claim against the estate is unsuccessful, the court may rule that the losing party is liable for legal costs.

Action list

- ☐ Select your team of competent, trusted professionals for estate planning: an estate planning lawyer, your accountant, and your financial adviser.
- ☐ Think about the outcomes you'd like to achieve through your will, and make preliminary notes.
- ☐ Cover all possible scenarios, including your own death, the death of your partner, and the unlikely event of both of you passing away simultaneously.
- ☐ Work with your team to draw up your notes as a will, and a memorandum of wishes in plain language (to be reviewed by your solicitor for consistency with the will) to minimise any potential misunderstandings.

2

Tips for making an effective will

An effective will minimises the risk of challenges and contestation, considers what the beneficiaries will receive after taxes and duties, and makes things as simple as possible for your executor. That's not as easy as you might think, so let's look at key issues to be aware of before you draw up your will.

These include:

- the relevance of asset ownership
- which assets will be distributed as part of the estate and which separately
- the characteristics of different types of assets
- the various types of trusts that may be relevant to inheritances
- Centrelink issues, particularly relevant to anyone receiving the age pension
- property considerations
- extra needs for your will if you have dependent children.

Understanding asset ownership

When preparing your will it's important to appreciate which assets form part of your estate and can be disposed of via your will, and which assets are not part of your estate and therefore cannot be bequeathed by the will. You must understand the nature of those assets because they may well have different characteristics that could be very important when your will is being prepared.

Usually, one of the first questions a solicitor will ask you at your appointment for a new will is whether you own any property as joint tenants or tenants in common. I am told that a blank look is the typical response; most people just do not know, and if they do know, don't understand why it matters. So let's look at why asset ownership is so important when drawing up your will.

Estate assets are assets held:

- in your name only
- as tenants in common.

Non-estate assets are assets held:

- as joint tenants
- in discretionary trusts
- in superannuation.

Estate assets

Items that you own in your own name are bequeathed through your will. These may range from household goods to a share portfolio.

Anything you own as a tenant in common has a fixed treatment upon death of one of the owners: the survivor/s continue with their present holding, and the deceased person's share passes to their beneficiaries following the terms of their will.

Tenants in common is the usual way that brothers and sisters or friends hold property. In this modern age where divorce and remarriage is commonplace, we find more and more couples are holding all their property as tenants in common, to allow their own children to have their share. If you want your surviving spouse to continue to live in a home you held as tenants in common, you could take advice about inserting a provision in your will that would enable it, and avoid the children of an earlier marriage forcing your new husband or wife out of their home.

Non-estate assets

Anything you own as a joint tenant, in a trust, or in superannuation (which is technically also in a trust) cannot be bequeathed via the will. Life insurance is also disposed of according to its own rules, and not through the will.

If a couple hold assets as joint tenants, and one dies, the entire asset automatically passes to the other holder irrespective of the terms of any will. This is called the "right of survivorship". This is the usual way that a husband and wife hold the family home. Obviously, you should not hold an asset as joint tenants unless you wish the other holder to have your share if you die first.

It's important to think about the ownership if you are considering making a bequest of a specific property or proposing a testamentary trust in your will. Because a jointly owned property automatically goes to the surviving owner and is not part of your estate, it cannot pass to a testamentary trust. This could produce unwanted results. You can change joint tenancy to tenants in common, just make sure you take advice about the tax and stamp duty consequences of doing this before you act.

CASE STUDY

David and Susan have both been married before. He has two children from a previous marriage, and she has four. As they don't intend to have any more children, they hold assets as tenants in common. This enables David's children to have half the proceeds when he dies and Susan's children to have half the proceeds when she dies. The position would be different if the assets were held as joint tenants and David died. David's half would pass directly to Susan and how much she then gave to David's children would be at her discretion.

> When David and Susan are preparing their wills, they need to think about what should happen when one of them dies. Is the intention for the survivor to remain in the house as long as it's convenient for him or her, or is the preference for the property to be sold and the proceeds split between the beneficiaries? A life tenancy is seldom a good option, for reasons I'll discuss later, but the survivor could be given the right to buy the property on the death of their partner, or even occupy it for a specified time. This is a complex area, and you'll need expert advice.

In addition, most older couples have joint bank accounts, which can save a lot of hassle when one of the partners dies, because the account continues as normal. You just need to take evidence of their death to the bank and then the account will revert to the survivor. It's also becoming common, as Australia's population ages, for an older person to have a joint account with one of their children. This can be invaluable when the older person passes away and there are ongoing bills to pay for the deceased's estate.

Such a joint account provides ease of access, but if other siblings do not even know of the existence of this account, there could be some tension if the older person dies and the bank account — which may have a considerable balance — passes automatically to the joint-owner sibling. Therefore, make sure there is full disclosure within the family: that all the children know of this joint account and its ultimate purpose of paying expenses such as probate costs, solicitor fees, rates and the other bills that keep coming after a person passes away. Keep in mind that the more transparent you keep the finances, the less chance there is of squabbles later.

If property is held in a trust it is also a non-estate asset, and the trust deed should be carefully considered before drafting your will. The succession plans in the trust deed need to line up with your will and your wishes. Assets held in a trust cannot be bequeathed in your will because it's not you personally who owns them, but the trustee of the trust fund. Your wishes could be carried out by either amending the trust deed or inserting a clause in your will — but only if the trust deed permits. Again, this is a complex area and you should consult a specialist succession lawyer about it.

Understanding asset types

There are numerous asset types, each with their own characteristics to consider: Do they offer the possibility of capital growth and/or loss? Are they income-producing, and does any income have tax advantages? How liquid are they — how quickly can you cash in your investment, in whole or in part?

Let's think about the main ones.

- **Cash:** By this I mean money in an account of some sort — not the cash in your pocket or down the back of the sofa. Cash has no chance of capital growth, and the interest carries no tax advantages. However, there should be no chance of a fall in value (other than the slow erosion of inflation) and, unless the money is in a term deposit, you should be able to get it back at short notice. At date of death, the value should be certain.
- **Property:** This includes residential and non-residential property, and your own home. It has the potential to provide capital growth and may provide rental income, but the income carries no tax advantages and is taxed at your marginal rate. It can be valued for estate purposes, but the true value cannot be known until a sale has been made and completed. The main trouble with property is that it is not liquid and usually cannot be sold in part. This can cause complications when drawing up a will — if there are numerous beneficiaries and you wish to leave a property to one of them, some of the others are likely to feel resentful.

- **Shares:** Essentially, this refers to any investment in which you own a defined stake, or share, of the total.
  - *Listed shares.* These are shares listed on a recognised stock exchange, which can be sold or bought at short notice. This means the valuation could normally be known on any day you choose. They have good potential for capital growth, and if the asset is a share in an Australian company, the income may be franked, which makes the income tax-free for many recipients. The disadvantage of shares is that their price can be volatile, and if you pick a dud you may lose the money you invested in that share altogether.
  - *Unlisted shares.* These are shares that are not listed on a stock exchange; for example, a family company, or a public company that has invited certain investors to buy shares, but has not yet become a listed public company. Their value is often uncertain, because they are infrequently traded, and they can be difficult to dispose of because buyers may be limited.
    - A common use of unlisted shares is as shares in a company that has no assets and is purely the trustee of a self-managed superannuation fund. Although they have no monetary value, they can have immense power as the shareholders are controlling the superannuation fund.
    - The appointment and/or replacement of directors is specified in the company's constitution. You should review this with your accountant, financial

planner and solicitor. Typically, a deceased shareholder's executor replaces that shareholder for the purposes of voting. This means that, if it is a company with a sole director/shareholder, the executor can vote for themselves to become its director.

- *Managed funds.* These are investment vehicles in which you do not have control of the assets, because they are held by the fund itself. They are extremely common; for example, property syndicates and share trusts run by big fund managers.
  * You must give notice to the fund manager of intention to redeem. Each fund has a set turnaround time: one fund in which I invest has a seven-day turnaround, another requires 45 days. Valuation is struck at the redemption date, not the date you give notice.
  * The delay between notifying intention to redeem and actual redemption can complicate cash flow planning when administering an estate.
  * A fund tax statement for the year ending 30 June is required for the final estate tax returns, but is often not available until at least four months after 30 June.
  * If you or the estate own managed funds, check with the fund manager and note their redemption policy details for your executor.

A READER'S TALE

My nan and mother have passed away in the last couple of years. Whilst I was not the executor (the Public Trustee was for both) I have a comment to make. My nan had money in MLC, who issue their financial/tax statements yearly in September/October each year. My nan died in August. The statement issued shortly after her death, of course, was for the previous financial year. We then had to wait an entire extra year to obtain the statement for the short period she lived in a new financial year: i.e. her estate was held up for a year. The Public Trustee could not hurry them up. I do not understand why they could not have issued a statement earlier. I did ring them, but of course they would not speak to me because as soon as a person dies the enduring power of attorney becomes null and void. It seemed an unnecessary hold-up for the paperwork and was stressful.

A READER'S TALE

When my father had terminal cancer and knew his days were numbered, he visited a solicitor to change his will. He wanted to make donations to a couple of cancer charities and, having a good knowledge of his financial position, nominated generous donations in his will. At the time the solicitor questioned his decision, suggesting that his wife could donate to the charities later, in her will. My father refused, saying that the charities needed the money now.

My father passed away a few weeks later and my mother started the lengthy process of applying for probate and then executing his wishes. During this period, the UK stock market (where my father had invested his wealth) took a dive. My mother sold all his shares to honour his legacy, but it left her with very little to live on.

My siblings and I appreciate my father had honourable intentions, but he wouldn't have wanted my mother to have to worry about making ends meet, like she did. My message to others would be never to put fixed monetary amounts in a will, unless that money is not subject to possible decline. It's better to allot using percentages, or allocate on an asset basis.

Trusts and your will

Trusts often play a major part in the estate planning process. In this section, we will discuss the various types of trusts and how they can be used — however, the main element of any trust is that the assets are not owned personally, they are owned by the trust.

This makes them particularly effective if you wish to leave money for the use of certain beneficiaries, but you don't want them to have full control of how that money is spent. These may include children, as well as family members who have some kind of incapacity.

They can be effective in protecting assets from creditors, and can be highly tax-effective, as the right kind of trust can distribute income between the beneficiaries of the trust with the aim of reducing the overall income tax.

Put simply, a trust is an obligation binding a person (the trustee) as the legal owner of some specific property (the trust property) to deal with that property for the benefit of a person (the beneficiary).

There are a range of trusts in the legal landscape but, in this book, we will stick to express trusts — that is, trusts that are created intentionally by a trust document. They may be *inter vivos* trusts, which are created by a trust deed, or testamentary trusts, which are created by a will.

Parties to a trust

- The **settlor** is the person who creates the trust relationship in an *inter vivos* trust, by paying a nominal sum to the trustee. Once that transaction has occurred, the settlor has no further involvement.
- The **trustee** is the legal owner of the trust property. They carry out the day-to-day administration of the trust, including management of the trust finances, buying and selling assets, and preparing paperwork. In many cases, including my own, the trustee is a private company that owns no assets and whose sole function is to act as trustee.

  The trustee exercises discretion in determining how and when to distribute the trust's income or capital among the beneficiaries based on the trust deed's provisions. They are bound by their fiduciary duty and must act in the best interests of the beneficiaries.
- An **appointer** (or **guardian** in some states) is relevant only to discretionary trusts, which are explained below, and they are critical to the management of the trust.

It is the appointer who holds the power to remove the trustee and appoint a substitute or additional trustee. This can be a crucial role if there are family disputes. This role grants them significant control over the trust's administration and decision-making. The appointer's primary responsibility is to appoint a suitable trustee, who will manage the trust assets in accordance with the trust's objectives.

Types of trusts

Discretionary trusts

Discretionary trusts (often called family trusts) are probably the most common type of trusts in Australia, because many small businesses operate through them. They provide the utmost flexibility and are very effective for tax minimisation and protecting assets.

They are not specifically an estate planning tool like a testamentary trust, but they are very useful over your lifetime. Keep in mind that a major element of estate planning is deciding how family assets will be split when a significant family member dies. Trust assets cannot be bequeathed in your will because they are not your personal possessions, but you may well own shares in the company that is the trustee, and those shares can be left in the will.

If this is your situation, take advice. When my wife and I were reviewing our wills, the solicitor pointed out that our trustee company had just two shares, but we have three children and it would be difficult to divide two shares between three people. The solution, which cost virtually nothing, was for the trustee to issue four more shares, making a total of six shares, which could then be easily divisible by three.

CASE STUDY

Ian and Nina have a beach house and a share portfolio — both are assets of their discretionary family trust. They have four children. Because they don't own the assets personally, they can't leave them directly to the children, but they could make a direction to the trustee of the fund as to where they would like the assets to go on their death. Depending on the advice they receive, the children may decide it is probably better to simply keep the assets in the name of the trust after their parents die. This is why a trust is so flexible.

A discretionary trust does not die when you do — it has a legal life of its own. This is why expert advice is essential when you are doing your estate planning. You may think the trust should be wound up and the assets sold on your death, but this could have stamp duty and capital gains tax implications, and it's possible that your children would prefer to receive specific assets — the legal term is *in specie*. The best outcome may be to arrange your affairs so that control passes to the intended beneficiaries on your death and then they can do with them what they will. This is particularly effective if the family owns rare assets, such as a beach house in a great location. Holding the asset in the trust means there is no property to be transferred when anybody dies, and it may well stay in the family for many decades.

CASE STUDY

Mr and Mrs Lee have a substantial superannuation balance, and due to the punitive tax treatment on balances over $3 million, which will start in 2026, decide to move $2 million out of their superannuation fund into a family trust. They do this via an *in specie* transfer of $2 million of listed index funds. This will be the only asset of the trust and is also the couple's principal asset, apart from their home and their superannuation. Let's assume the index fund averages 4.5% growth long term and 4.5% income (80% franked). After 12 months the income should be $90,000, plus franking credits of $36,000.

The growth will vary from year to year, but if it achieved the long-term average, the growth would be $90,000 as well. This would be subject to capital gains tax, but not until the asset is sold, either by the will-maker or their beneficiaries.

The sum of the dividend plus the franking credits ($126,000) would be added to the Lees' taxable income for the year. This means that $63,000 would be added to each person's taxable income. The tax on this would be about $11,000 each, but they would have the benefit of $18,000 each in franking credits. Under current legislation, the excess of $7000 would be refunded to them.

If the Lees had a substantial income in their own names, and their children and grandchildren were beneficiaries of the family trust, it may be possible to stream income down through the trust to beneficiaries in a lower tax bracket. This is particularly appropriate if the grandchildren are aged 18 and over, and studying.

If you have a discretionary trust, you should look at the schedule of the trust deed to ascertain who the appointer is. The appointer has control of the trust, and it is at their total discretion who receives any benefits from the trust.

The schedule may make provision for a replacement appointer to be named at the time of the original appointer's death, or the trust deed may make provision for the current appointer to make provision in their will appointing a new appointer of the trust upon their death. If such a provision exists, you may want to make provision in your own will to appoint someone as your replacement appointer, thus giving them control of your trust assets when you're no longer here.

If there were specific assets held by the trust that you would like to go to certain individuals, you could consider a letter of wishes stipulating what you would like to happen in respect of those trust assets. It's not legally binding, but in most cases has a highly persuasive effect.

Unit trusts

Unit trusts are also income-splitting devices, but they lack the flexibility of the discretionary family trust. They are used when you want to keep the interests of the beneficiaries separate. This may be because the investors are unrelated, or because different members of the same family are involved as investors.

CASE STUDY

Bob decided to buy a property in partnership with his two brothers, Terry and James. They had different amounts to contribute and wanted to safeguard their share of the asset. The property cost $900,000. They put in $500,000 between them, and took out a loan of $400,000 in all the brothers' names to complete the purchase.

	Initial investment
Bob	$250,000
Terry	$150,000
James	$100,000
Total	**$500,000**

After talking to their accountant, they decided to set up a unit trust that contained 90 units worth $10,000 each ($900,000) and issue them in proportion to the funds contributed.

	Initial investment	Unit trust shares
Bob	$250,000	45 units (50%)
Terry	$150,000	27 units (30%)
James	$100,000	18 units (20%)
Total	**$500,000**	**90 units** (100%)

The main point to realise is that there is no discretion here at all. Suppose the net rents of that building were $44,000 and the interest was $24,000, leaving a taxable profit of $20,000. That $20,000 had to be distributed to all the unit holders in proportion to their unit holding, as follows.

	Initial investment	Unit trust shares	Profit distribution
Bob	$250,000	45 units (50%)	$10,000
Terry	$150,000	27 units (30%)	$6,000
James	$100,000	18 units (20%)	$4,000
Total	**$500,000**	**90 units** (100%)	**$20,000**

The figures work out neatly, and it's all nice and clear, but the result is not the best for tax-saving purposes. For example, it may not suit Bob if he is already in the top tax bracket, for he will lose 47% of his share in tax.

It would have been a better strategy for Bob to buy his shares in the unit trust in the name of his discretionary family trust. Certainly, the unit trust would still have had to distribute the $10,000 of income, but because the beneficiary is the discretionary family trust, it could have passed the income down to its own beneficiaries more tax-effectively.

Unit trusts certainly keep the affairs separate, but this lack of flexibility can cause problems. They are sometimes used where lack of trust makes people wary of using a discretionary trust, but if that is the key reason, they can be combined with discretionary trusts to excellent effect. The price of flexibility is a little extra complexity.

CASE STUDY

I had a client who owned a valuable building in the name of a unit trust, of which the beneficiaries were his four children (three sons and a daughter) who each had a 25% share in a discretionary family trust. All the beneficiaries were earning high incomes until his daughter's husband had a serious accident and was unable to work. Since the accident the daughter and her husband have had little income, and the perfect solution was to divert 100% of the income from the trust to them. This can easily be done with a discretionary trust but cannot be done through a unit trust.

Fortunately, my client had prevented the problem in advance by using the discretionary family trusts as the unit holders. Each sibling's family was a potential beneficiary of the other's trusts. So they simply flowed the income down through the unit trust to each family discretionary trust, which redistributed it to the daughter.

Testamentary trusts

Testamentary trusts are one of the favoured tools in estate planning. It's a fact of life that relationships can fail, and it is not uncommon for people to lose money through scams, going into business, or getting caught up in bad investments. When you leave money to your beneficiaries through a testamentary trust, the beneficiaries may have the use of that money, subject to certain conditions, but it is not their own property. This gives them some protection against relationship breakdowns, creditors and lawsuits.

They are also a very effective tool for minimising tax.

Just be aware that testamentary trusts involve set-up costs and ongoing administration costs and therefore may not be appropriate for smaller and uncomplicated estates. It could be that a simple will is sufficient, as testamentary trusts can be onerous and expensive to maintain.

This section is just a brief explanation of testamentary trusts — if you think you need one, proper legal advice is essential. There are many things to consider.

CASE STUDY

A couple had four children. One was a builder in a business that was suffering cash flow problems and material shortages, the second was a gambler, the third was in a rocky relationship, and the final one was a highly paid professional in the highest tax bracket.

If the family had left their money to each of these children individually, what are the likely outcomes? The builder may have gone bankrupt and the creditors would have taken all the inheritance, the gambler would probably have lost it all, a major chunk of the inheritance could have walked out the door when the rocky relationship finally broke up, and the professional would have lost much of their inheritance to tax when the extra income unexpectedly boosted their already high income. Furthermore, the professional was keen to put asset protection in place to protect their inheritance from a possible professional liability suit.

It was fortunate that the couple got good advice and left the money to four testamentary trusts.

> This meant that creditors could not touch the builder's inheritance, the gambler's money was protected for him, and the departing spouse was not easily able to grab a share of the inheritance.
>
> The professional's inheritance was protected from lawsuits, and they were enabled to invest the money in ways that suited their situation and minimised tax.

The set-up of a testamentary trust depends on the circumstances. When our children were young, our wills provided for testamentary trusts with instructions to the trustee to pay expenses such as education fees, private health insurance, medical expenses, and to provide funds for a motor vehicle or home deposit if the trustee thought that was appropriate. Now the children are middle-aged and through them we have grandchildren. We are still using testamentary trusts, but they now have much wider discretion to do what they think is best with the money.

A testamentary trust is not like a discretionary family trust. A testamentary trust is written into the will and sits dormant until the will-maker dies. At that stage, the testamentary trust comes into effect. A will may also provide for a testamentary trust without making it mandatory – depending on the terms of the will, the executors and the primary beneficiary of the will may have the ability to choose whether a testamentary trust is appropriate. Once again, this is a matter for legal advice.

Tax treatment

One of the key advantages of a testamentary trust is its potential for tax minimisation. Income generated by the trust is generally distributed to beneficiaries, who are then taxed individually based on their own personal tax rates. This can be advantageous as it allows for income splitting, enabling beneficiaries with lower marginal tax rates to receive income and pay tax at a lower rate.

In Australia, earnings by minors from "unearned income", such as income from gifts, is taxed at punitive rates. The first $416 is tax-free, but if more the entire balance is taxed at the top marginal rate. However, income distributed from a testamentary trust to a minor or earnings on an inheritance received by a minor are treated as "excepted income" and taxed at ordinary adult rates.

CASE STUDY

Jules and Jim wanted to leave $50,000 to each grandchild and sought advice on how best to do it.

They found that if they simply asked their children to gift $50,000 to each grandchild out of their own inheritance, the grandchildren, under 18 would be heavily taxed as the investment earnings would be "unearned income". For example, if that $50,000 earned $2,000 a year, the total tax would be $900, because the first $416 would be tax free but the next $891 would be taxed at 66% then the balance of $693 would be taxed at 45%.

If instead they change their will to state that $50,000 was left directly to each grandchild or a via testamentary trust, it becomes excepted income from an inheritance. The grandchildren would pay zero tax, the first $18,200 would be tax free then only 16%, up to the next threshold of $45,000.

Overall, the tax treatment of income from a testamentary trust in Australia offers potential advantages in terms of tax minimisation and income splitting. It provides flexibility and opportunities for beneficiaries to manage their tax obligations effectively, while enjoying the benefits of the trust established for their benefit. Note, however, that the tax treatment of income from a testamentary trust can vary depending on the specific circumstances and provisions of the trust. Complex rules and anti-avoidance measures are in place to prevent misuse of testamentary trusts for tax purposes. It is advisable to seek professional advice from a tax expert or a qualified legal professional when establishing and managing a testamentary trust.

Trusts for people who cannot control their inheritance

Most parents believe that it's best to treat all children equally, but if one or more of the children has an intellectual disability, a substance or dependency issue, or are simply unable to handle money well, there are a range of specialised trusts to cater for their situations. Let us give you some examples, so you have an idea of what tools may be available to you.

Capital protective testamentary trusts

A capital protective testamentary trust is a valuable estate planning tool that aims to protect and preserve the assets of beneficiaries while providing them with financial security. They are set up as part of the will like a normal testamentary trust, but state that the executor or another independently nominated person will control the trust on behalf of the child. The person has a wide range of powers, which could include buying a property for the child, paying rent, or even providing the funds for a rehabilitation centre if required.

A capital protective testamentary trust can also be structured to provide ongoing financial support to beneficiaries while preserving the principal capital. This is achieved by granting the trustee discretionary powers to determine the amount and frequency of distributions based on the beneficiaries' needs and circumstances. The trustee can consider factors such as their age, health, education, and financial requirements when making distribution decisions.

The primary objective of a capital protective testamentary trust is to safeguard the inheritance of beneficiaries, especially in situations where they may be vulnerable to financial risks or mismanagement. This type of trust provides a layer of protection by allowing the testator to specify how the trust assets should be managed and distributed over time.

A capital protective testamentary trust offers tax advantages. The trust is taxed as a separate entity, allowing for potential tax savings and flexibility in distributing income among beneficiaries. The trustee can employ various strategies to minimise the tax liability, such as distributing income to beneficiaries in lower tax brackets or using franking credits.

Special disability trusts

A special disability trust (SDT) allows families and carers to provide for the long-term care and support of a person with a severe disability. It offers a range of benefits and exemptions to ensure the financial security of individuals with disabilities, while preserving their eligibility for government assistance programs.

The first step in establishing an SDT is to determine whether the beneficiary meets the eligibility criteria. To qualify, the beneficiary must have a severe disability as defined by the *Social Security Act 1991*. This includes physical, intellectual, or psychiatric impairments that significantly affect their daily activities and require substantial and ongoing care. The beneficiary must be either under 16 years of age or eligible for the disability support pension.

Once eligibility is established, the next step is to appoint a trustee. The trustee is responsible for managing the trust's assets and making decisions in the best interest of the beneficiary. The trustee may be an individual or a corporate trustee, such as a trustee company. It is crucial to choose a trustee who understands the complexities of managing a trust and is capable of fulfilling their duties diligently.

Funding the SDT is a critical aspect of the set-up process. Contributions to the trust can be made through various means, including cash, real estate, investments, or life insurance policies. However, it is essential to consider the impact of these contributions on government entitlements. Services Australia provides guidelines on how assets and income held within the trust are assessed for means-testing purposes. Seeking professional financial advice can help navigate these complexities and maximise the benefits of the trust.

Once the SDT is established and funded, it is necessary to notify Services Australia. This notification allows the department to assess and confirm the trust's compliance with the legislative requirements for social security purposes. It is crucial to keep accurate and up-to-date records of all transactions and activities related to the trust, to ensure ongoing compliance.

An SDT offers several benefits, including income and capital gains tax exemptions, assets test concessions, and the ability to protect the beneficiary's eligibility for government support payments. However, be aware that the trust is subject to ongoing obligations and reporting requirements. The trustee must lodge annual tax returns and provide regular updates to Services Australia regarding changes in the trust's circumstances.

Centrelink and your will

Most retirees receive some form of income support. If that's the case, and you are in a relationship, it is important to consider your will's impact on the surviving partner. The most common mistake is for couples to leave each other everything, and push the surviving partner over the lower singles threshold for receiving the age pension.

See page 257 for details about how working with Centre-link rules may affect the financial planning aspects of estate planning.

Property and your will

Key terms	Explanation
Life interest	A life interest gives the right for the beneficiary to live in a property for the rest of their life, or for a specified period. It may be subject to a range of conditions, such as keeping the home in good repair and paying relevant outgoings. When the life interest ends, the asset is given back to the estate. – Under a ***life tenancy***, the beneficiary may also be entitled to any income generated by the property, if they are not living there. – Under a ***right to reside***, the beneficiary is unable to obtain income from the property.

Key terms	Explanation
Remainderman	Whoever is entitled to the interest in the property after a life interest has ended.

Providing a home for your spouse and extended family

A common concern for many couples is what will happen to the surviving spouse when one of them dies. The family home is often their major asset, and they may wish to arrange their affairs so the surviving spouse can keep living in the property while the property stays in the estate. This is known as a "life interest". The will may need to be drafted so that the survivor can't be forced out of the property by circumstances such as a dispute over the estate, or one of the children's relationships breaking down.

There are several instances in which a will-maker may consider including a life interest in their will. They may wish to ensure their children are not disadvantaged if the surviving spouse enters into a new relationship, or may have children from a previous relationship who could also benefit from the estate. Or, if the will-maker has elderly parents who are incapacitated or not financially secure, a life estate may be a suitable option to take care of them.

The main issue to be considered is whether the holder of the life interest has the financial capacity to maintain the residence and be financially comfortable during their lifetime.

It is also important to ensure that your will is drafted carefully to avoid any ambiguity.

A "life tenancy" is essentially the right for your surviving spouse, elderly parent or adult child to live in the family home and also be entitled to any income generated by the property for the rest of their life, or for a specific period of time. When the life tenancy ends, the asset is then given back to the estate and distributed to the ultimate beneficiaries. Consideration needs to be given to whether the life tenant (should they wish to live in the house and not rent it out) has access to funds to pay for the upkeep of the property.

Previously, life interests used to be cumbersome and inflexible and it was not possible for the holder of the life interest to rent or sell the house to finance a move to aged care.

Thankfully there are a range of more flexible options now and it is important that you discuss these with your lawyer.

A "right to reside" is often presented as an alternative to a life tenancy. It means that the will-maker gives a person the right to live in the home, subject to a range of conditions such as keeping the home in good repair and paying relevant outgoings. However, the resident is unable to obtain income from the property, and when the right ends, either on their death or move into aged care, the asset is returned to the estate for distribution.

As outlined earlier in the book, there is a historical principle that a spouse should be provided with secure accommodation, and failing to do so could give rise to a claim for further or better provision by the surviving spouse (a family provision application). Nonetheless, both these options should be approached with care, as they create a long-term commitment for the beneficiaries that may limit the options for the deceased person's estate, particularly if the property holds significant financial value. It is also necessary to consider the long-term financial impact on the holder of the life estate, or the deceased estate itself, of maintaining the property. This drain on estate funds could affect the ability to distribute assets among other beneficiaries, potentially causing conflicts or legal disputes from the surviving spouse or disgruntled beneficiaries. It is important to carefully assess the overall impact on the estate and consider a range of options to balance the interests of all parties involved.

Another option is a discretionary testamentary trust, with the surviving partner and the children as beneficiaries.

Yet another is to consider the other assets of the estate: many people now have significant superannuation, in addition to the family home, and the super could be used to balance the distribution between the surviving spouse and the children of the first marriage. However, if you are relying on superannuation to even out the distribution it is important to regularly review your estate planning, as the super balance would normally reduce once the member starts to draw a pension from the fund. Also, expert taxation advice is required, as super left to children over the age of 18 could be treated as a payment to a non-dependant for tax purposes, unless they meet the relevant requirements for financial dependency or interdependency.

Outright gifts could be another option, if the estate is large enough. For example, the family home could be left to the surviving spouse, and an investment property and superannuation given to the children of the first relationship. A much simpler option is for the family home to be sold and the surviving spouse given sufficient funds to buy a new place of their own. This, of course, depends on whether the family wants to keep the family home.

This can be a complex and challenging situation, with many things to consider. However, as with all these options, it is essential you consult closely with your accountant, financial planner and lawyer when estate planning.

Taking care of dependent children

If you have young children when you make your will, you should consider who will care for them if one or both parents die. Therefore, parents of minors should include a clause appointing a guardian in the event of their death. If one parent dies, an appointed guardian has to make decisions with the surviving parent regarding the care of the child or children. Should any dispute arise in relation to parental responsibility or questions of long-term care of the children, then it would be necessary for that to be resolved by the court. Guardianship of a child can be changed by court order.

The will-maker should communicate with the proposed guardian and discuss how they wish their child to be raised, including matters such as religion, culture, schooling, etc. The will-maker should also ensure that their will includes a provision that gives the guardian access to sufficient funds to carry out the wishes of the parent.

The interplay between state and federal legislation as it relates to parental responsibility and testamentary guardianship is complex, therefore you should obtain expert advice before appointing a testamentary guardian in your will, to ensure it is the right thing for your family.

I cannot stress highly enough that this is a complex area, and this chapter provides nothing more than a brief overview. You should always seek expert advice, because getting it wrong can be costly. A good financial adviser will think about the taxes you pay today, into the future and upon your eventual demise. Intergenerational wealth and tax planning done well can have immense value, so be sure to encourage your advisers in the legal, financial, and taxation fields to collaborate effectively and openly.

Action list

- ☐ Review your draft will with the greater knowledge you have gained from this chapter, with your full team and with your executor/s and beneficiaries, if appropriate.
- ☐ Plan for the wellbeing of your children if they are under 18, specifying who will make decisions regarding their welfare, who will care for them, and whether the caregiver should receive financial compensation.

3

Enduring powers of attorney

Let's now move to the next essential element in planning your estate: appointing somebody to act on your behalf if you are not able to do so. This is called a power of attorney. The big difference between this and making a will is that the will takes effect after you die — a power of attorney ceases when you die.

Don't fall into the trap of thinking you won't need to have an attorney until you are old — the need can strike at any time. Giving somebody a power of attorney, like drawing up a will, is something you should do now.

All states and territories have their own laws regarding powers of attorney. To make it more confusing, the same effective documents may have different names, and use different terms, depending on the state in which you live. For example, an enduring power of attorney in Queensland can cover both financial and health decisions, but in New South Wales an enduring power of attorney covers financial decisions only, and a separate document appoints an enduring guardian for health decisions.

An "enduring power of attorney" endures even after you have lost mental capacity. A more limited version, which would lapse if you lost mental capacity, is called a "general power of attorney". The distinction is important, and you should discuss this with your solicitor.

This chapter also covers the advance care directive, a separate document setting out your preferences for health care if you are unable to make a decision at the time. This is essential if you want to prioritise quality of life over length of life.

Key terms	Explanation
Principal / Donor / Adult	The person who gives another person the right to act on their behalf.
Attorney / Donee / Agent	The person who is given the right to act on another person's behalf.
Power of attorney (PoA) / General power of attorney	The document by which the principal appoints an attorney and sets out what the attorney is authorised to do. An attorney can do no more than the principal who gives the power of attorney. And this type of power will lapse if the principal loses capacity. For this reason, it should be avoided in estate planning.
Enduring power of attorney (EPA)	A special power of attorney that lasts for the life of the principal, or until revoked by the principal. Provided the principal was of sound mind when the power of attorney document was executed, any later loss of mental capacity of the principal is not relevant. It is this type of power of attorney that is most relevant to estate planning.
Guardian	A person granted authority to make decisions about medical, personal and lifestyle decisions, if the principal is unable to make those decisions for themselves.

Function of a power of attorney

There are three areas over which an attorney can be given authority:

- legal and financial decisions
- medical treatment decisions
- personal and lifestyle decisions.

Within each area, authority can be given at various levels, ranging from the right to make withdrawals on a certain, specified bank account, to the right to do almost everything you can do yourself.

Simple rights may be given through specific mechanisms, e.g. the right to operate a bank account is usually given simply by signing one of the bank's forms. Broader powers are conferred on another person or people when you execute a power of attorney document.

Unfortunately, there is no uniform Commonwealth legislation surrounding powers of attorney or enduring powers of attorney; all states and territories have their own laws regarding powers of attorney. So remember that this information offers only a general guide, and that the terms we have used may not match those used in your state or territory. Make sure you engage a solicitor who practises in your state or territory.

The enduring power of attorney (EPA) lasts for the life of the principal, or until revoked by the principal. Provided the principal was of sound mind when the power of attorney document was executed, any later deterioration in the state of mind of the principal is not relevant.

When you need a power of attorney

It doesn't matter how young you are, accident and illness can strike without warning at any time and suddenly create the need for an EPA.

How would you cope if you suddenly broke your arm, or became seriously ill? Would your regular bills be paid? Who would withdraw money from your bank account to pay medical expenses and other unexpected costs? If you were severely injured, and needed to sell your house to buy one that was more suitable, who would be able to sign the contract and transfer documents? If you were holidaying overseas when sickness or accident struck, could anyone access your bank accounts if you needed money quickly?

To cover situations like these, you should appoint at least one other person to act on your behalf. This person is often called your agent, or in legal language, your attorney.

Australia has one of the longest life expectancies in the world, and dementia is growing more common as life expectancies increase. It is projected that by 2050 over 900,000 Australians will suffer from some form of dementia. As dementia progresses, there inevitably comes a time when legal and testamentary capacity are lost, and your EPA and will must be in place before this occurs. Fortunately, it usually progresses slowly, giving families time to prepare. But many people move to avoidance instead of preparation, leaving themselves, and their families, at risk of huge problems down the track.

Any loss of mental clarity, whether it's mild cognitive impairment or an early diagnosis of dementia, is a definite warning to prepare or review your EPA.

If you don't make an EPA while you can, there are only two options — either you will fall through the cracks in society's systems, or someone who cares about you and is aware of your situation will have to apply to the appropriate tribunal in your state to appoint someone to be your administrator (to make financial decisions) and/or your guardian (to make personal and health decisions). One person can hold both roles, if suitable. The application process can be both costly and time-consuming, and will typically be made by a family member, close relative, close friend or trusted professional (such as a lawyer or a financial adviser) — would you want to foist that onto them?

Don't fall for the myth that your spouse or next of kin can make financial decisions on your behalf in the absence of an EPA. That's a dangerous delusion: without an EPA, the only decision-maker will be one appointed by a tribunal.

Capacity

It is vitally important to put an EPA in place long before it is needed, because you cannot give someone an EPA if you don't have the capacity to do so.

Capacity, for the purposes of a power of attorney, involves the principal having the ability to understand the nature and effect of the decision, make that decision freely and voluntarily, and be able to communicate that decision clearly. The principal needs to be "in sound mind", essentially another term for having sufficient capacity, to appoint an attorney to manage their financial and personal affairs.

As discussed previously, there are differing levels of capacity depending on the type of document or decision you are entering into. The threshold for executing an EPA is higher than for a will. It is therefore important for the witness to your signature to also assess your capacity to enter into it. If it is not witnessed by the solicitor who prepares the document, who will already have discussed it with you in detail, the witness will normally read the document in some detail and ask you questions about it. This process assesses your ability to take in information, apply a level of reasoning to it and then to demonstrate your understanding of such an important document by answering some questions.

Unfortunately, not all eligible witnesses realise the importance of the above assessment, and it often does not take place. There have been numerous instances where an elderly person whose capacity is impaired has been taken to a local shopping centre and plonked down before a JP who has, without any questions, witnessed the document.

Provided the principal is of sound mind, an EPA — unlike a general power of attorney — will stay in force until revoked by the principal, or until their death. If the attorney becomes of unsound mind, the EPA is automatically revoked.

SMSFs

An EPA is especially important if the family has a self-managed super fund (SMSF). The regulations require all members of the fund to be trustees, but also prohibit a person without sufficient capacity from being a trustee of the fund. In the event of a member/trustee losing capacity, all decisions would need to be made by a person appointed by a tribunal, if no EPA has been executed by the member who has lost capacity.

Validity

When you are preparing a power of attorney, take the time to make sure it complies strictly with the law, so that it will be valid. The EPA must be signed by the principal and properly witnessed, and it must also be signed by the nominated attorney/s. That is, the appointment must be both given and accepted. Your attorneys may sign independent of you, and each other, and after you, as the following story illustrates.

CASE STUDY

Maria had given an EPA to her two children to operate jointly or separately. Years later, she got dementia and when the time came for her to move to a nursing home, the children took the EPA to her bank to withdraw $500,000 for the bond. The bank refused to accept the form, because they noted that the attorneys, the two children, had signed before the principal, the mother. The form was invalid because the essence of the form is that the principal gives power of attorney to other people. In this case they had signed the document before they had been given the power.

My legal friends tell me the matter could have been simply solved by having the attorneys re-date and sign the document, but the bank did not accept that course of action.

This is a good example of the wisdom in taking the EPA to any organisation you think might need it well before it's needed. They normally take some time to peruse and accept it. In my own case, I was given a power of attorney from my son who lives in America, and when I took it to his bank to transact business, I was told it would need five days for approval.

Preparing a power of attorney

A power of attorney is a simple document that sets out the name and address of the principal, the name and address of the attorney, and the powers given in the document to the attorney.

We will cover choosing an attorney in detail soon, but for now you should realise that whoever you appoint may be responsible for some significant financial decisions. You should be confident that they:

- understand their duties and responsibilities as your attorney
- are capable of undertaking this role
- are prepared to act in your best interests
- can and will keep accurate records.

An EPA usually contains the following:

- an appointment of one or more persons as attorney/s
- an authority to do anything the principal lawfully authorises the attorney to do
- a declaration that the power of attorney will continue even if the principal becomes incapable.

The EPA must be signed by both the principal and the attorney and witnessed by an appropriate person. The witnessing requirements vary from state to state, but the form itself is usually a good guide.

You can obtain a standard form online and do it all yourself, but I suggest you have one drawn up by your solicitor. A good time to do it is when you are having your wills prepared or updated. There are many facets to estate planning, and signing do-it-yourself documents can sometimes cause you many problems that a solicitor's guidance could have avoided.

The EPA should be kept in a safe place with your other estate planning documents, so it can be accessed quickly if necessary. If you intend to use it for buying and selling property, a stamped copy should be registered in the Titles Office or Real Property Office — or whatever it is called in your state. Your solicitor can do all this for you.

When the EPA document is prepared, it can take effect immediately, or only in the event of certain circumstances triggering activation of the power. Such a circumstance could be when, in the written opinion of your treating GP, you are unable to make decisions for yourself. If this is written into the EPA document, the bank (or other organisation) will only approve the attorney's access to the accounts once they have seen an appropriate written medical opinion. Each organisation has their own processes and it is best to check what they require.

If you wanted extra safeguards, you could request two written opinions of your lack of decision-making capacity. If your attorney is trying to activate the EPA with nefarious intentions, this would normally put a stop to them — it may be possible to convince one GP to falsely confirm incapacity but convincing two would be much more difficult.

Remember, an EPA can be used as a "licence to steal" by a dishonest person, because when you appoint an attorney, you most commonly give someone the power to do anything that you can do. Once the EPA becomes active, the document enables the attorney to stand in your shoes and sell property, withdraw cash or close bank accounts. Although it is possible to limit the powers you give your attorney, this also carries high risks, as you have no way of knowing what may need to be done.

Financial abuse is one of the most prevalent forms of abuse for people aged over 65 years and abuse of a power of attorney is one of its key methods. We explore this in more detail on page 147.

It is essential that you appoint someone you trust, who is likely to be competent to manage your affairs, and that you carefully consider the scope of the power that you give them. If they do abuse your trust, once the money is gone, it can be an expensive legal process to get it repaid.

CASE STUDY

Eva, an 85-year-old widow, went to hospital for a minor procedure. She had no family and had appointed her neighbour, Tony, as her attorney. In the hospital she developed a urinary tract infection, the symptoms of which often include temporary confusion and loss of mental capacity.

She was assessed as having impaired capacity and Tony arranged for her to move into a locked dementia ward in an aged care facility. Once she was admitted, Tony did not visit her, but proceeded to withdraw sums of cash from her account.

When the infection cleared, Eva regained her mental capacity, but then spent the next six months in guardianship tribunal hearings to prove her capacity before she was discharged from the aged care facility. On her return home she saw a "For Sale" sign on her house. With the assistance of a community legal service, she was able to revoke Tony's power of attorney and take the house off the market. Unfortunately, she was not able to recoup the monies taken by Tony, who had moved away and could not be located.

Types of powers

An EPA for legal and financial decisions is likely to need to deal with paying day-to-day bills, renewing insurances, and maintaining any property the donor owns. If the donor is older, their attorney may also need to deal with the sale of the family home and/or putting together documents for admission to aged care.

To decide to admit someone to residential aged care, however, they will need authority to make personal and lifestyle decisions, or be directed by someone who can.

As for medical treatment decisions, it is important to understand that life-prolonging treatment will always be offered unless you have made an advance care directive that clearly specifies what kinds of treatments you reject and in what circumstances. And it must be easily available in case of emergency. Your attorney for health matters will need proper authority backed up by the correct paperwork, if they are to be effective.

Remember, authority can be given with few or many caveats, but since you don't have a crystal ball, it is usually best to give more freedom rather than less to your attorney. If you know someone who is both competent and trustworthy enough, and who is prepared to take this responsibility on for you, you are very fortunate.

Amending your power of attorney

It is not possible to amend an EPA, only to revoke it. An EPA lasts until revoked by the principal or until the principal dies. The laws vary a little from state to state. So to amend an EPA, you revoke it, then create a new EPA.

Parties to a power of attorney

Principal / Donor / Adult

When you ask someone to accept your EPA, you are asking a big favour from them.

It's important for you to realise this, and help to make their life easier if the EPA ever becomes active.

READER TIPS: KEEP THE FAMILY ON SIDE

The more transparent the family financial situation, the less chance of disputes. Often, one family member has been running the family finances for years and may forget the value of the experience they have acquired over that time. One of the greatest legacies they can leave is educating the younger members of the family both in general financial principles and specifically in the way the family finances are run.

A great way to do this once the kids work is to emphasise the importance of earning rate on the final balance of the superannuation fund. By working with them on the right mix of assets for your super fund, and explaining the way money works, you can really help the children gain a good knowledge of finance. As time passes, they can become more involved in complex family structures such as family trusts and a self-managed super fund.

Often the problem is that nobody takes the time to work together to get a good knowledge of the way the family finances work. Don't neglect it — it could be one of the best uses of time you've ever made.

A READER'S TALE

After my husband was incapacitated by a stroke, I needed to sell some of the huge number of shares he had acquired — mostly through dividend re-investment. But he is no longer able to tell me anything about them, and I didn't have a clue how it all worked. Our accountant told me I needed to get someone to sort out the paperwork, for "if and when anything happened". But it already had! In all the stress, I had a fall and I've had to move in with my daughter. She also has my husband's EPA, and now she is phoning and emailing constantly, trying to get to grips with it.

Keep in mind that up-to-date records make the difference between a hellish, drawn-out process and a relatively painless process for an attorney (or executor). And how difficult it can be for anyone to get the records if insufficient paperwork has been kept.

No delegation

A power of attorney cannot be used to delegate a power. To illustrate, if you held a power of attorney for a Qantas pilot it would probably enable you to operate her personal bank accounts, and even buy and sell shares and property. But it would not allow you to put on her uniform and fly the aeroplane. The pilot is appointed by Qantas, and the power to fly their planes cannot be delegated to another person by anyone but Qantas.

CASE STUDY

Henry unexpectedly became incapacitated. He was the sole director of his own business and his brother Bill had expected that he could use the power of attorney to run the business while his brother was unable to do it. He was not allowed to.

A company director is a person appointed by the company, and that appointment cannot be delegated by the director to another person. Solicitor Brian Herd points out that if the director is also a shareholder of their company, that shareholder can appoint an attorney, and the attorney can exercise all the rights and powers of that shareholder. Therefore Bill, representing Henry in his role as shareholder, could exercise the right of that shareholder to appoint a new director — this could be Bill himself.

Financial institution issues

A mortgage broker told me about a couple who had given each other EPAs years ago. Now they were much older and living on an acreage property. She had just been admitted to a nursing home and they needed funds. The EPA was still valid, but she had now lost capacity and was not able to change it. They were trying to get a reverse mortgage over the property to help them get the funds they needed, but only one lender was prepared to take on the acreage property where they lived. The problem was that this bank's rules prohibited such a loan, unless the EPA had a specific provision whereby either party could sign a mortgage on the family home. They therefore refused the loan. When I last spoke to the mortgage broker, he said the matter was being referred to a tribunal. This again highlights how different institutions may have different policies.

Attorney / Donee / Agent

Attorney responsibilities and duties

An attorney must:

1. exercise their powers diligently and honestly to protect the interests of the donor
2. avoid undertaking any transactions that may involve a conflict of interest between themself and the donor, unless there is specific authority for it in the document
3. keep their own money and that of the donor strictly separate
4. keep proper accounts and records of how the donor's money and other affairs have been handled. Good records are wise, for both parties' protection, and the attorney may be asked to produce them. If an attorney causes the donor a loss by failing to perform their duties properly, they may be required to compensate the donor.

Choosing your attorney

A major issue for many people is who to choose as your EPA. Your spouse is often your first choice, but they may predecease you, or also lose capacity as they age. This can be got around by appointing some or all of your children, if you have any, as alternative attorneys. But you must consider family conflicts that may arise. It's sad, but we regularly hear of cases where one child ingratiates themselves with the ageing parent and talks them into giving power to that child only. Next thing you know, they are changing the locks to prevent other siblings making "unwanted visits" — and continue down the path of taking total control. This is elder abuse.

The same considerations apply to choosing an EPA as to choosing an executor — you need someone trustworthy, organised, competent, available, willing, and preferably one who has a good relationship with family members and is younger and healthier than you. It does seem a lot to ask! It can be tricky if you have children: Do you appoint them all? Maybe one lives overseas or is estranged. But choosing only one or two may make the others feel excluded from having any say in your future finances, medical treatment or lifestyle.

If family friction is a possibility, you may consider appointing a non-family member, such as your lawyer or accountant, as your EPA. They are not under any obligation to act, and would normally charge for their services, but this is likely to be a lower cost than a major family dispute.

You may also decide to appoint more than one EPA. Multiple attorneys can work in several ways.

- **Severally:** Any of your attorneys can act for you independently.
- **Jointly:** All of your attorneys must approve any action made on your behalf. This can quickly become unworkable, particularly if they do not live in the same area, as all would have to sign any documents.
- **Consecutively:** Your EPA may pass from one attorney to another, in the event of the first being unable or unwilling to act when the time comes.
- Other options include appointing multiple attorneys with any two to sign …

As you can see, this is a very complex situation and getting it wrong can have enormous costs. This is why it is vital, where wills and EPAs are concerned, to take advice from a lawyer who is a specialist in estate planning. The cost of that advice is likely to be minuscule when compared with the potential problems.

In my own affairs, my wife is my only attorney, but if she is unable to act, the power automatically flows to our three children.

Appointing a professional as an attorney

If there is nobody in your family or friendship circle that you feel can undertake the role of enduring power of attorney, or you want to appoint a backup, there are professional organisations or people whom you can appoint as your attorney.

You could appoint:

- a private trustee company
- a solicitor or accountant
- the Public Trustee (in your state or territory).

You must contact the person or organisation before appointing them as your attorney to ensure that they consent, and to clarify their fees and charges. As professionals, they are entitled to charge for their services.

Please note that in some states the Public Trustee incorporates the Public Guardian, and in others they are separate. For example, in NSW the Public Trustee and Guardian can be your attorney for personal and financial decisions, but in Queensland the Public Trustee can only be your attorney for financial decisions and the Public Guardian must be appointed separately for personal and health decisions.

Asking your solicitor or accountant to act as an attorney can present some professional and ethical challenges, in the form of conflicts of interest, so don't be surprised if they decline your request to act as your attorney.

Most standard power of attorney forms do not include a clause enabling the EPA to charge for their services. If you choose to appoint a professional or organisation as your EPA, you must include an appropriate charging clause in the document. Make sure that professional services (e.g. compiling and submitting your tax return) and non-professional services (e.g. paying your bills) are not charged at the same rate.

Private trustee companies and the Public Trustee in your state or territory should have their own schedule of fees and charges for your consideration, and these may offer a basis for a detailed conversation with your solicitor or accountant about how they charge to be your EPA.

Generally speaking, "out of pocket expenses" are payable to the attorney even without a charging clause. This should be discussed with the professional attorney so there are no surprises.

Accepting an appointment as attorney

You may think it's a great honour if somebody asks you to be their attorney, but before you accept the role, remember it's a job that carries great responsibilities, and one that can easily lead you into strife, including legal action. Think carefully before you take on the role, and if you do, make sure the principal briefs you adequately.

As you can see, there may be considerable work and responsibilities involved, and if you don't take them seriously you may have problems.

If you decide to accept a power of attorney, keep good records; then if you do find yourself in a dispute, you have evidence to support your actions. Keeping minutes on a file is one good way to do this. They should preferably be contemporaneous.

For example, you may write:

> **25 March 2023.** *Mr Sharp (Mrs B's accountant) sent ATO assessment notice for a tax payment of $4,500. Paid direct to ATO by bank transfer from Mrs B's Commonwealth Bank acc.*

> **4 July 2023.** *Karen Smith (Ace Realty) phoned about Mrs B's investment house at 10 Premier Drive. Previous tenants vacated seven weeks ago and it is still vacant after extensive advertising. She suggested we drop the rent by $30 a week to $400 a week. Rang Alan Jones of XYZ Realty and Mary Collins of ABC Realty (other main agents in the area). Both confirmed $400 a week is realistic market figure. Approved the rent reduction.*

It can also lead to conflict — conflict of interest, and conflict with members of the family.

CASE STUDY

Let's assume that Mrs Brown is your neighbour. Her four children live interstate or overseas and she says it is comforting to have you close by. She is a lovely old lady, and you have no hesitation in accepting her request that she give you a power of attorney. Some years later she loses her mental capacities and her children help her move into a nursing home. There is no possibility of her returning to her old home. How do you handle the following?

Two of the children believe her home should be rented out. The other two don't want to see the family home "defiled" by tenants.

The eldest son, Tom, has a business that is borrowing money for expansion. He asks you to sign documents mortgaging the house as additional security for the loan. He assures you, "Mum promised to help if I needed it".

A daughter, Rebecca, has just divorced and is making a new life for herself. Mrs Brown's will divides all her assets between the four children equally. Rebecca feels the house should be sold now and the proceeds split four ways. Naturally this does not suit Tom, who needs the entire property to secure his loan. In any event, the other daughter, Helen, believes the property has great potential and it would be "a shame to sell it now".

> Let's look at the worst-case scenario. You think Tom is a very decent fellow and have no doubt that Mrs Brown promised to mortgage the house for him if necessary. Consequently, as attorney, you sign the documents needed to mortgage the house to secure his loan. Unfortunately, his business fails; the bank forecloses under its mortgage and sells the house at auction to help cover Tom's debts. The other three children sue you on the grounds that your action in permitting the house to be mortgaged was negligent.

Maybe I've painted a gloomy picture, and you think, "This would never happen to me". But every day we hear the most amazing stories of family feuds and reverses in family fortunes. Perhaps it won't happen to you, but accepting the role of attorney for friends certainly opens the door to a lot of possible heartache.

Also be aware that an EPA must not use their power to do anything to benefit themselves, or their family, unless specifically authorised to do so in the document.

CASE STUDY

You are an only child and your mother (a widow) gives you power of attorney. She becomes unable to look after herself and goes into a nursing home. The problem is her house. She wants to keep the full pension, but after she has moved out of it for a year Centrelink will treat it as an asset and she may lose much of her pension. If you put tenants in the house, the rental income could cause a reduction in her pension.

The obvious solution is for her to gift the house to you. You are the sole heir and you know this is what she would do if she was capable of doing it. However, she is in no condition to sign documents and you, wearing the hat of attorney, cannot gift the house to yourself as this is called a "conflict transaction". If you sell the house the sale proceeds must go in her name, and she will lose her pension.

I will discuss similar problems in a later section, but this one could have been simply solved if somebody else, maybe the mother's solicitor or financial adviser, had also been given a power of attorney.

Alternatively, a clause such as the following may be inserted in the EPA while the principal is still of sound mind.

> *I expressly allow and authorise my attorney to enter into transactions on my behalf where my interests and duty could conflict with my attorney's interest and duty in relation to the transaction. Without limiting the foregoing, I expressly allow and authorise my attorney to contract on my behalf with him/herself, each other, his/her/their relatives and entities in which my attorney may have an interest or control.*

Whew, that's a legal mouthful, isn't it? If you have an EPA in the house, why not stop reading for a few minutes and see if you can find that clause in it. If it's not included, and the principal trusts the attorney, it may be worthwhile having the document redrawn, although the principal's solicitor will probably advise against it.

Alternatively, if you have accepted an EPA and the duties become too onerous, it is possible to apply to your state's guardianship tribunal for an order that the Public Guardian or Public Trustee takes over the management of the person's financial and personal affairs.

Effective powers of attorney

When you are preparing a power of attorney, take the time to make sure it complies strictly with the law. It must be signed by the donor and properly witnessed. Then it must be signed by each attorney, and again, properly witnessed.

It must also satisfy the requirements of the institutions the attorney will need to deal with, which can be infuriating, diverse and archaic.

A solicitor friend tells me institutional requirements are often labyrinthine, outdated, resistant to change, and illogical, making for a nightmarish customer experience. Institutions are notorious for lacking a thorough understanding of the law, exhibiting a pathological aversion to risk, and obsessing over reputation management. Banks, for example, despite their discouragement of in-person interactions, and their pushing for online transactions, irrationally require the presence of attorneys for many transactions — if you can locate a branch that hasn't shut down.

For this reason, if you want to appoint joint attorneys, make sure there are no impediments, such as where they live, that may make it difficult for them to act.

A READER'S TALE

I am researching options for a friend who is managing the move of a lifelong partner into care as a result of dementia. She has a joint power of attorney with her partner's brother, who lives in another state. The power of attorney must be operated jointly.

From what I can establish so far, it is not possible to get a personal bank account that can be operated jointly (i.e. requiring two signatures for transactions) unless those people are in the same room using the same computer and type in their code, or if they visit a branch in person for each transaction. This seems ridiculous, in this day and age.

Risk of financial abuse

It would be remiss in a discussion of powers of attorney not to caution you about the risk of financial abuse that an EPA can lead to. Financial abuse is one of the most prevalent forms of abuse of people aged over 65 years, and abuse of an EPA is one of its key methods.

A UK judge several years ago coined the term "licence to steal" when referring to an EPA that was misused by the attorney, leading to significant financial loss for the principal. When you appoint an EPA, you are usually giving someone the power to do anything that you can do. Once it becomes active, the document enables the attorney to stand in your shoes and sell property, withdraw cash or close bank accounts.

Therefore it is essential that you trust the person/s you are appointing and carefully consider the scope of the power that you are giving them. Each of the ways to make it harder to misuse an EPA limit flexibility, or make things harder for the attorney, and we have discussed many of them already in this chapter, but they may still be worth doing. For example, you can appoint attorneys jointly, or as "any two to sign". Limiting the scope of powers, such as forbidding conflict transactions, also aims to reduce risk. Once money has been taken, it can be an expensive legal process to try to get it back.

Advance care directives (ACDs)

An EPA is vital, but it is not enough. I have never met a single client who did not express a wish to live as long as they were healthy, but not be kept alive if they had deteriorated to a level where life had become unbearable.

The document required to achieve this has different names in different states, but the general term is advance care directive (ACD). It sets out exactly what the donor prefers to happen if they reach a critical health situation. In Queensland, this document can also provide for the appointment of a power of attorney for health decisions.

You will need to involve a trusted medical practitioner in preparing your ACD. Not only are they required to sign the document, but you are highly likely to need their assistance to understand the medical terminology used in the document, and to express your wishes in a way that will make sense to those who may later be treating you.

Often, an EPA is prepared at a relatively young age, whereas the ACD is left until later. Be aware that the new power of attorney that can come into being when signed as part of the ACD automatically revokes the original power of attorney to the extent that it appointed a different attorney to make healthcare decisions. This can present problems, so make sure you check your EPA when you prepare an ACD, in case any changes are required.

The next challenge arises when the ACD is needed. It must be available, or it is useless. A friend found her terminally ill mother unconscious on the floor of her home. She was in no doubt that her mother's wish was to be left to die, but the ACD was in a safe deposit box at the bank. In its absence, the paramedics had no option but to revive her, even though it was against her express verbal instructions.

An ACD provides multiple benefits:

1. It gives clear guidance to family members and healthcare professionals about an individual's preferences regarding medical treatment. It enables an individual's healthcare wishes to be respected and followed, even if they are unable to communicate their desires. An ACD outlines what treatments an individual
   - would like to receive, such as palliative care, hospice care, or any other comfort measures
   - would **not** like to receive, including life-sustaining treatments such as ventilation, resuscitation, and feeding tubes.
2. It eliminates the burden of decision-making from family members during a difficult and emotional time. When a loved one is seriously ill or injured, family members are often called upon to make critical decisions about their medical care. This can be daunting, particularly if family members do not know what that person would have wanted. An ACD alleviates this burden and allows anyone to ensure that their loved ones are not forced to make difficult decisions on their behalf.

3. It provides peace of mind to both the individual and their family members. Knowing that one's healthcare wishes are documented, and will be respected, can relieve anxiety and stress. It also provides assurance to family members that they are following their loved one's wishes, even if they disagree with them. By having an advance care directive, an individual can be confident that their end-of-life care aligns with their values and beliefs.

4. It can help prevent family conflicts. When family members are forced to make decisions about a loved one's medical care, disagreements can arise that cause rifts in family relationships and create lasting tension. An ACD makes it much less likely for medical care to become a source of conflict or tension among family members.

5. It allows individuals to make their own choices regarding their end-of-life care. It enables them to retain control over their medical treatment, even if they are unable to communicate their preferences. This directive can ensure that an individual's medical care aligns with their own values and beliefs, rather than with external factors such as family members' wishes or the medical community's views.

6. It is a legally binding document that ensures an individual's medical wishes are respected. There are instances where the treating medical professional is not obliged to follow the ACD, but that is only in circumstances where it is contrary to good medical practice.

A READER'S TALE

Soon after he turned 81 my father had a heart attack, which the hospital patched up beautifully. But he experienced severe hypoactive delirium, which was not surprising, given his dementia. He had strong views about not being given life-prolonging treatment, and had an ACD he'd discussed in detail with the family, and which the hospital received within hours of his arrival.

Even so, he was in hospital for three long weeks. We arrived one morning to find him intubated. We were told that, although this was uncomfortable and he didn't want it, he would be even less comfortable without it. It took another day to be able to meet with the appropriate doctor to secure his release. During this time, Papa pulled out his tubes and was forcibly restrained while they were reinserted. It was very upsetting.

The doctor reviewed the ACD with us, asking if we could cope with his palliative care at home; we had to fight to follow his ACD. With hindsight, palliative care is really tough and I appreciate the doctor's intention. After just one week, Papa died at home, as he'd wished. Knowing that we gave him the end-of-life care he wanted has been a great comfort in grieving him. Without the ACD, and confidence in what it said, we couldn't have done that for him.

Action list

- ☐ Appoint an enduring power of attorney (EPA) for financial decisions, and personal and lifestyle decisions, plus an enduring guardian for health decisions.
- ☐ Additionally, document an advance care directive (ACD) covering resuscitation, organ donation, and your preferred place of care during the natural dying process. Ideally, engage in open discussions with your family, allowing them to contribute and comprehend your intentions before you are no longer present to guide them.
- ☐ Provide certified copies of your EPA and ACD to those appointed, and to any other relevant people, such as your GP, home carers, or a residential aged care home.

4

Minimising tax on your estate

A major part of estate planning is arranging your affairs to maximise your beneficiaries' inheritance, which means minimising tax. I apologise in advance if some of this appears complicated: in some situations, it's impossible to reduce complex rules to simple language. The main goal in this section is to make you aware of the implications of your choices. We will explain things in detail, but bear in mind that in some areas it can get extremely complex and you should always take expert advice.

These are the main points to understand:

- There are specific tax exemptions for the principal place of residence (the family home) that are well worth understanding.
- Keeping good records is a must. It will save you time and money.

- The amount of tax payable depends both on the person or entity that holds the assets at date of death, and on the recipient's tax status.
- When deciding which beneficiary should get certain assets, their own tax status is of critical importance.
- Death usually does not trigger capital gains tax — this liability is passed on to the beneficiaries.
- Capital losses are lost on death.
- If overseas assets are left to you, the tax rules of that country may apply.
- If you leave assets to an overseas beneficiary, there can be complications.

The family home

The family home is a major asset in most estates. Its tax treatment on death depends on four factors.

1. Is the house a pre-CGT asset — acquired before 20 September 1985?
2. Is the house a post-CGT asset — acquired on or after 20 September 1985?
3. Can the house be wholly or partly covered by the main residence CGT exemption?
4. How is the title held?

Let's discuss each of these in detail now.

Pre-CGT asset

The tax treatment is simple — it will remain CGT-free, even if it has been rented out.

If it was held as joint tenants, the survivor will continue to hold their original half of the property as a CGT-exempt asset, but the half they "inherited" becomes a post-CGT asset from date of death, if that is after 19 September 1985.

When the survivor dies:

- provided the house was covered by the survivor's main residence exemption at their date of death, the beneficiary will inherit the property at its market value at the date of death of the surviving owner and they will be entitled to the two-year CGT-free period in which to sell the property.

- if the property was not covered with the survivor's main residence exemption when they died, their original half still gets full CGT-exemption, and their beneficiary has two years to sell CGT-free. However, for the half they "inherited" after 19 September 1985 there will be some CGT, calculated from a cost base of market value at the date of death of the original joint tenant.

If it was held as tenants in common, the CGT treatment is the same as above, but the beneficiary of the deceased's share of the house may not be the co-owner. The property is distributed in accordance with the deceased's will.

CASE STUDY

Jack and Jill married late in life when they met after their original partners had died. They bought a home in 1984 for $200,000, but because they wanted to leave their share of that home to their individual families, the property was bought as tenants in common, with each having a 50% share. When Jack died, his share of the house was distributed in accordance with his will to his children. The children tried to force Jill to sell the house. Jill challenged this but eventually lost after a legal battle over three years.

Jill's half of the property was still a pre-CGT asset in her hands, so no CGT was payable on her share of the sale proceeds. As more than two years had passed since Jack's death, the children would be liable for CGT on any capital gain made from market value at date of death to the sale price. However, there are some concessions that may help them reduce this.

- They could apply for the ATO's discretion to extend the two-year CGT exemption period on the grounds that the estate was challenged.
- They may have also lived in the house and covered it with their main residence exemption.
- As Jill was Jack's spouse, Jack's children's half of the property can also be covered by Jill's main residence exemption beyond the two years up until the day she moves out.

If the land was bought before 19 September 1985 but the house was not built until after that date, there would be two separate assets. The house would have to be treated as a post-CGT asset, but the land would retain its pre-CGT status. A valuation would be necessary to apportion the sale proceeds between the house and land.

Post-CGT asset

If the property is owned as joint tenants, there is no resetting of the cost base to market value at date of the death of the first spouse, even if it has always been their residence. The surviving joint tenant will acquire the deceased's share of the property at the deceased's cost base, but can cover it with the deceased's main residence exemption for any period it qualified in the deceased's hands. When the surviving owner eventually dies, their heirs will inherit the property at market value at date of their death if it is being covered by the survivor's main residence exemption at time of death.

The key difference with tenants in common is that with each owner's death the cost base of their share of the family home is reset to market value at the date of their death.

The difference between joint tenancy and tenants in common is not a big issue if the property has always been covered by their main residence exemption, but it's a different situation if the home was initially used as a rental and sold within the surviving owners' lifetime.

CASE STUDY

Bill and Marie bought a beach house but rented it out for two years before they retired and moved there. They lived in it for three years before Bill died, then Marie continued to live in the property for a further five years before she sold it. The CGT treatment of the property will vary depending on how the title is held.

Tenants in common: Marie inherits Bill's share with a cost base of the market value at the date of his death and is deemed to have acquired it at that date. This means treating each half as a separate asset acquired at different times. She has owned the half she inherited from Bill for five years, all of which was covered by her main residence exemption, so no CGT is payable on that half. But the half she has always owned, for a total of 10 years, had been rented for two years, so is not fully covered by her main residence exemption: 20% of the capital gain on that half will be taxable, but of course she would get the 50% CGT discount.

Joint tenants: Marie inherits Bill's share as if she owned it in the time he owned it. As both half ownerships were used in the same way she can treat this as one asset, but because there is no market value reset on Bill's share the two years of exposure to CGT affects both halves. Therefore 20% of the whole gain over the 10 years is subject to CGT before the 50% discount is allowed for.

The CGT payable is at least double what it would have been if they had owned it as tenants in common. A couple can change from joint tenants to tenants in common without CGT or stamp duty consequences providing the ratio of ownership remains at 50% each. If there is some CGT exposure on your home, it is worth considering this. As always, take advice from your accountant before acting.

For the market value reset to apply in the case of tenancy in common or sole ownership, it is not necessary for the deceased to be living there when they die, provided the dwelling is entitled to be covered by their main residence CGT exemption at the time they die. The six-year absence rule can be used to continue to cover the property with their main residence exemption for up to six years after they move out if it is being used to produce income, or infinitely if it is not producing income.

Continuing the main residence exemption after death

The deceased's main residence exemption can continue to protect the property from CGT for two years after death, providing the property is covered by the deceased's main residence exemption at the time of death and the property is not being used to produce income — unless the deceased was absent and the six-year rule applied.

If this is the case, you have at least two years in which to sell the deceased's home without attracting CGT. Note that the relevant dates are the dates of ownership — as defined by settlement, not when the contract was signed. If there are problems leading to a delayed settlement, you may be able to extend the two years you have to sell without triggering CGT. Further, during this two-year period the property can be rented out without affecting the CGT concession.

This two-year period can be extended at the ATO's discretion when there are delays beyond the control of the executor. Examples of this include if the will is challenged, COVID delays the sale, or probate is delayed. It does not cover extra time to do up the property to get the best price — the delay must not be a choice.

If the deceased's spouse continues to live in the house, or someone is given a life tenancy under a will, it can continue to be covered by the deceased's main residence exemption during this period of occupancy, even though it exceeds two years. It is exempt from CGT for as long as this person lives there. But keep in mind that it is the deceased's main residence exemption that is being extended, not the occupants'.

From the day the life tenant dies or moves out, the CGT clock starts ticking. There is no resetting of the cost base to market value when the occupant dies. The capital gain is calculated from the original deceased's date of death (DOD). Although their main residence exemption can cover the property from DOD until the life tenant dies, it is a pro rata calculation based on the number of days the life tenant lived there compared with the number of days between the life tenant's death and sale of the property.

Section 118–192 ITAA 1997 provides a great little trick to give you more time to sell. If you can get the property to earn income as soon as the life tenant dies, you get to reset the market value of the house again to the market value at the date it first earned income, with no CGT applicable before that date. This will not only reduce your record keeping to a much shorter period — it may also reduce your CGT to zero by the time you factor in the selling costs.

Held by a trust or a company

If your home is owned through a company or a trust, your death will not affect the ownership of that property, as the entity that owned the asset has not died. However, if it is a unit trust and you hold the units personally, your estate will have to deal with the ownership of the units. It's the same situation if you hold shares in a company.

Your estate planning should include a plan for transfer of the shares in the company. In my own case, we have a company that acts solely as trustee of our family trust and our self-managed super fund. When we were doing the regular update of our estate planning, the solicitor pointed out that we have three children, but the family trustee company had only two shares. This could have caused complications when one of us died and the children became shareholders in the trustee company. As touched on in Chapter 2, the problem was easily fixed: the company issued four more shares, so the company now has six shares, which divide easily between three children. There was no cost to do this, and no CGT issues because the company was merely a trustee, it did not own any assets. It would have been a different story if I tried to issue more shares in a company that owned an asset such as property.

Bear in mind that holding your home in a company or a trust will prevent you or your estate from taking advantage of the CGT concessions for main residences.

Additional points

If you have a right to occupy, or are a life tenant, the property does not transfer to your estate, it transfers to the remainderman.

If the deceased had been a foreign resident for tax purposes for over six years immediately before death, none of these concessions apply. These issues are covered in more detail later in this chapter. Australia is always going to retain the right to tax Australian real estate, no matter where in the world the owner resides.

Record keeping

When I was researching this book, I phoned accountant Julia Hartman and asked her what the biggest challenges were when handling deceased estates. She replied, "Lack of record keeping and fights between beneficiaries". We will focus now on record keeping, because good records is one of the best gifts you can give your executor and beneficiaries. If records are not kept properly, it may delay the estate and cost a great deal to re-create the records.

Julia considers this so important that she has developed a package of spreadsheets for this purpose, with full instructions, which is available from ***www.bantacs.com.au/shop-2/getting-your-affairs-in-order-made-simple/*** Type "Noel" into the voucher section of the shopping cart for a 20% discount.

Key terms	Explanation
Date of death (DOD)	The documented date of death, as specified on the death certificate.
***in specie* bequest**	Gift of an asset transferred directly from your estate to the beneficiary, rather than sold and the cash transferred to the beneficiary
FIFO	First in, first out — a way of allocating sales of items, such as shares, that have no specific individual characteristics. The assumption is that items are sold in the same order in which they were bought.

Key terms	Explanation
Presently entitled	An individual's legal right to receive income or assets from a trust or estate in the present. If presently entitled, the individual has an immediate and enforceable claim to the benefits, without any conditions or restrictions. It grants the beneficiary control over the assets, including their distribution and use. The concept of present entitlement is vitally important in determining the tax implications and timing of distributions within an estate plan.
Section 99B	The section of the *Income Tax Assessment Act 1936 (ITAA 1936)* that applies when an Australian taxpayer is a beneficiary of a foreign trust, from which money or another asset is paid or applied for their benefit. Trust assets may include cash, land, shares and other assets.

Record keeping tends to be one of these jobs that we never get around to. And the natural tendency when the subject is raised is to think, "I'll get round to it later, when I have time". Worse still, you may think, "It's not my problem!" But just think: if it feels all too hard now, how difficult is it going to be for your heirs and executor to sort out when you are not around to answer questions? Do you really want the ATO to be a major beneficiary of your estate?

Records are particularly important for reducing capital gains tax. In many cases, you can reduce your taxable capital gain by claiming quite a wide range of expenses, but only if you have the records to substantiate your claims.

If you need help with record keeping, you might like to start with the appendix, Keeping the right records.

Records for pre-CGT assets

If you acquired an asset before 20 September 1985 it is not subject to CGT, but you need to have a record proving that it is a pre-CGT asset in your hands. This is usually simple to establish with real property — the Titles Office should have acquisition details. It's not so easy with listed shares and units in managed funds. The share registry may

— or may not — have a record, and in many cases they will charge you a fee to extract the information.

CGT can also get quite complex. Take, for example, a pre-CGT asset that was owned jointly. If you survive your co-owner, the half that you inherit from them will be a post-CGT asset in your hands, so you will need to record the market value of their half at their DOD and keep records from that point onwards.

If you own pre-CGT land, and build on that land or make significant improvements to it after 20 September 1985, the improvement will be considered a separate post-CGT asset from the original land. You will need to keep separate records for the building/improvements.

Records to establish any CGT discount for non-residents

From 8 May 2012, those who are non-resident for tax purposes lost their right to the 50% CGT discount. This is why it's so important to have good record keeping tracking the dates you have lived overseas.

Furthermore, you will lose your main residence exemption right back to the day you first bought the property if you die overseas after living overseas for longer than six years, or sell your Australian home while you are a non-resident of Australia for tax purposes. Coming back to Australia for a holiday and selling while you are here won't help — you must genuinely take up residency again.

CASE STUDY

Mary owned her home in Australia for 30 years, then went overseas to help with a new grandchild. After a couple of years, her health started to fail and she decided to stay. Mary sold her Australian home to buy something near the children overseas. Australia taxed all her capital gain over those 30 years — she was not eligible for any main residence exemption at all. When inflation is taken into account, as well as the astronomical gain of Australian property prices, her original purchase price is probably less than 10% of the sale proceeds.

As it was her home and she didn't see any of this coming, she had not kept detailed records. The capital gain will probably be 90% of the sale proceeds. She will get the 50% discount on most of that gain — just not for the time she lived overseas — but she will also be paying tax on that gain at non-resident tax rates, which means no tax-free threshold.

Even if Mary chose not to sell the property because the tax would eat up a lot of the money she'd get, it doesn't solve her problem unless she gets healthy enough to move back to Australia. Here's the tricky part: if she passes away after living overseas for six years or more, Australia can still take all that tax money from her estate, even though she never came back.

Good record keeping would have allowed her to increase the cost base by the many improvements she made to her home over 30 years. Further, if she had purchased it after August 1991 she could increase the cost base by holding costs such as rates, insurance, interest, and repairs and maintenance. Her taxable gain would have been much less.

CGT records for collectables and personal use assets

Capital gains tax is triggered when you dispose of an asset, whether by sale or gift. The ATO deems gifts as a sale based on the current market value.

It applies to "collectables" (which include artwork, jewellery, antiques, and valuable coins, postage stamps, and books) with a purchase price of $500 or more, so just about all jewellery is caught in the net. And it is not just taxable if you sell it to a third party — CGT is also triggered when you gift something, with deemed sale proceeds based on the current market value.

For personal use assets (which include boats, electrical goods, furniture, and household items, except those classed as collectables), CGT only applies if the asset cost is more than $10,000.

The passing of a loved one, like your wife or grandmother, leaving wedding and engagement rings to you, serves as a prime example. Should you opt to pass those rings on to your daughter, CGT must be paid as if they were sold at their current market value. So maintaining receipts for both personal items and investments is equally crucial.

For estate executors, it becomes important to consider whether the jewellery originally cost more than $500, as it may be subject to CGT despite being held for personal purposes. The acquisition date plays a significant role. Key acquisition dates are 19 September 1985 and 16 December 1995.

Determining the original cost of the jewellery may pose a challenge. How could Mum have known to keep such records when it was a heartfelt gift? Nevertheless, the responsibility of maintaining records rests with the taxpayer. Failure to prove the original cost of the jewellery could result in CGT being paid on the entire sale proceeds, without any cost base being subtracted.

Furthermore, this rule extends to heirlooms that are centuries old. Even if they were acquired before the introduction of CGT, any change of ownership after 19 September 1985 starts the CGT clock, unless their market value at the time of transfer was less than $500.

CGT records for shares and units in trusts

If you are involved in a dividend reinvestment plan, make sure you record the number of shares received and the cash dividend forgone for each reinvestment. The number of shares is a great check to make sure you have not missed any. Dates are also important for the CGT discount.

Keep all the documentation you receive regarding any mergers, demergers, rollovers, bonus issues, etc. The trap for listed securities is that the first share you purchase will be considered the first share you sell (FIFO basis). There is no ability to just average out the cost. So if you have sold a portion of your holding, it is important that your record keeping carefully allocates that sale to particular shares.

The same rules apply to cryptocurrencies — a CGT event is triggered when you switch from one currency to another.

Record keeping for property

Your home

The CGT main residence exemption is not a right — a number of taxpayers have had to fight the ATO for it. A good example is Ms Summer, who lived in a shed the ATO didn't consider habitable. After enduring criticism in court from the ATO about her living standards, being unmarried and not cooking, at least the judge ruled in her favour, stating that it is not for the ATO to judge where people make their home, only that they have made their home there. This principle didn't, however, help the Erdelyis family — in their case the judge ruled in the ATO's favour, because of the lack of furniture in the house and its small electricity bill. The judge ruled that their main residence was really at their daughter's house, where they spent a lot of their time. Then there was the minister of religion whom the ATO ruled couldn't cover his home with his main residence exemption because he spent four days of the week at the manse next to the church.

If the house you live in is not in your name, you can't cover it with your main residence exemption unless it is being held in a bare trust for you.

There are many reasons why you should keep all the normal CGT records for your main residence just as if it were an investment. It gives you flexibility, so if you end up with more than one property that qualifies, you can choose to apply your main residence exemption to the property with the highest capital gain. Consider this situation: you have two houses and have lived in both, but have also used both as rental properties. You decide that the house you have lived in the most is not the one you want to cover with your main residence exemption, because its cost base can be increased by all the holding costs while you are living there. But to do this, you must have the records to prove it.

The cost base for properties acquired after 20 August 1991 can be increased by any holding costs that have not otherwise been claimed as a tax deduction. Holding costs include rates, insurance, interest, body corporate fees, repairs and maintenance, which could even include cleaning materials and lawn mowing. This is particularly appropriate for family beach properties that were never rented — all expenses incurred since acquisition can be added to the cost base to reduce CGT. The big items here are interest, land tax, insurance, and rates. All of these are relatively easy to obtain historical records from the supplier while you are alive, but far more difficult for your executor.

Investment properties, holiday homes and vacant land

Investment properties are most likely to have good records, because you are required to file tax returns each year and you need records to do this. The purchase costs, including all associated fees, are a major part of the base cost, but make sure you keep records for anything that you have not otherwise claimed as a tax deduction.

When it comes to investment properties acquired after 13 May 1997, you will also need to track the building depreciation that you have claimed as a tax deduction, as this amount will reduce your cost base.

With non-rented holiday homes and vacant land it is unlikely any of the holding costs would have been claimed as a tax deduction, so there is a great opportunity here to reduce your CGT by carefully recording everything — this includes interest, rates, insurance, repairs, improvements and maintenance, including cleaning and lawn mowing.

Inheritances from overseas

As the number of Australians born overseas grows, so do the implications for people who inherit from overseas residents — it could be as simple as receiving something when a parent dies. It's an extremely complex area and I recommend you take good advice if anything comes your way from overseas. All I can do here is to explain the system, in the hope it will lead you to ask better questions of your advisers. I am indebted to my good friend, Julia Hartman of BAN TACS, for most of the material on this topic.

How the estate is processed will make a big difference to how your inheritance is taxed. If the amount is more than $10,000, AUSTRAC will send details to the ATO, who will send you a "please explain" letter when the funds hit your bank account. By that time, it is too late to take steps to minimise any potential tax on those funds.

Even though Australia does not yet have a death tax, inheritance tax, or gift tax, other taxes can raise their ugly heads when a bequest from overseas is about to occur. This chapter covers the most common scenarios, but not all possible circumstances.

Firstly, what is an overseas estate? The simple answer is one that does not have an Australian executor. If just one of the executors is an Australian resident, the ATO will treat the estate as an Australian resident for tax purposes and may look for a share of the action. This is not necessarily to your detriment, but keep in mind that the countries of residence of the other executors and the deceased may be involved as well.

The most common situation is where the estate is not an Australian tax resident, but the beneficiary of the estate is.

In this situation, the tax treatment varies depending on what you receive and when you receive it. The explanations below apply to an Australian resident beneficiary of a deceased estate, where both the deceased and executor are non-residents of Australia for tax purposes.

An overseas property

First, the tax treatment depends on whether you receive the property before it is sold (an *in specie* distribution) or if the estate sells the property. It is quite common for beneficiaries to be unaware they have received the actual property in their own name, and to think it is still owned by the estate. If the will allows an *in specie* distribution, and if it is a good outcome for tax purposes, usually all the executor needs to do is change the name on the title documents from the deceased to the beneficiary or beneficiaries.

If the Australian beneficiary has capital losses, or there has been considerable capital gain since DOD, or the deceased owned the property before 8 May 2012, it is probably a better outcome for Australian tax purposes if the property is owned by the beneficiary when it is sold, not the estate. Transferring the property from the estate into the beneficiaries' names before that occurs should be enough, as long as it is not the estate that is selling the property.

If the estate sells the property, the capital gain made on that property by the estate is calculated in accordance with Australian tax law. The starting point is always the market value of the overseas property at date of death. Basically if you are entitled to 25% of the estate, you will be subject to tax in Australia on 25% of the capital gain as calculated in the hands of the estate. This will be taxed as normal foreign income, not capital gains, so you will not be entitled to offset any capital losses you may have or use any CGT discount. Further, you will be taxed on the gain made by the estate even if it was made in a previous income year to the income year you received the funds.

It's quite different for an Australian estate. If it was an Australian estate, and you did not receive the gain in the year the CGT event occurred, the estate would pay the CGT and no tax would be payable by you when you received the sale proceeds.

If it's a non-resident's estate, *Section 99B* is there to make sure all income and capital gains you eventually receive are taxed in your hands in Australia, in the year you receive them.

The trouble with *99B* is it treats the capital gain as income of a foreign trust, not actual capital gains. This means that you will not be entitled to any CGT discount or able to offset any capital losses you may have, against this gain. This problem can be avoided if you receive the asset instead. In fact, it may be a great outcome, as long as it is not an Australian property you are inheriting. If you receive an asset other than Australian property from a non-resident estate, Australia will not be able to tax any of the capital growth before you owned it, which is the date of the deceased's death.

Further, when you do sell you can offset any other capital losses you may have, and will be entitled to some CGT discount though it is unlikely to be the full 50% due to the property probably being owned by a non-resident for some time after 8 May 2012. This is an interesting twist for inheritances *in specie* from non-resident estates. When you do sell, your cost base starts with the market value at DOD, but your acquisition date for working out the days entitled to the 50% CGT discount remains the date the deceased acquired the asset.

Of course, you would need to consider the tax consequence in the country of the estate.

Inheriting in the estate or *in specie*

If there are no negative consequences in the foreign country, it may be better to transfer the property into beneficiaries' names before it is sold. Though if you intend holding for the long term, even gains made after DOD will still not be entitled to the full 50% CGT discount because for some of the period of ownership the asset was owned by a non-resident after 8 May 2012.

If the asset has low transaction costs, such as shares, consider selling quickly so there is very little capital gain over market value at DOD, and then buying the shares back, so that any future gain qualifies for the full 50% CGT discount.

CASE STUDY

Ben was a non-resident who had bought a foreign property for $100,000 in January 2000. When he died in January 2020, the property was worth $480,000. The estate sold the property in January 2022 for $500,000 (after deducting selling costs) and held onto the proceeds until January 2023, to make sure all of the estate's liabilities were met.

Ben's beneficiary, Lesley, who is an Australian resident, is entitled to 50% of the estate. In the end the other assets were enough to cover the liabilities, so the 2023 distribution was made up of the sale proceeds of the foreign property, i.e. $250,000 to Lesley.

Unlike the situation with Australian estates, *Section 99B* captures the capital gain made by the estate in the 2021–2022 year as normal foreign income of the Australian beneficiary in the 2022–2023 year. The gain won't be much, because the first element of the cost base will be the $480,000 market value at DOD plus some holding costs, let's assume $2,000. The capital gain is calculated as $500,000 – $482,000 = $18,000 x 50% (two beneficiaries) = $9,000 to the Australian beneficiary.

Section 99B does not allow this to be treated as a capital gain, so there can be no CGT discount or offsetting of losses — it is just foreign income taxed at marginal rates plus Medicare.

Consider if the entire property were transferred to the two beneficiaries in June 2021, before the sale. This would mean that half the property was owned by an Australian resident. When the beneficiaries sold the property in January 2022, the resulting gain would be reported on Lesley's 2022 tax return, not as regular foreign income from a trust, but as a capital gain. Although the gain amount would still be $9,000, there is the potential for some CGT discount and offsetting of any capital losses due. This approach differs from the previously discussed scenario where the sale occurred before the beneficiary ownership took effect.

The interesting twist is the calculation of the portion of the 50% CGT discount that will apply. Even though the cost base is reset to market value at DOD, it is the deceased's acquisition date that is used for the purposes of apportioning the discount.

Non-residents are not entitled to the 50% discount for any ownership period after 8 May 2012. The discount is apportioned by days entitled to the discount versus days not. Using a simplified example with months: the discount applies from January 2000 to May 2012 (148 months) and then again from January 2020 to January 2022 (24 months). That's 170 months out of the total 264 months, meaning the beneficiary gets 64% of the full 50% discount, or roughly 32%. This lowers the taxable gain from $9,000 to $6,120.

This approach is only possible because the property was transferred to the beneficiary before it was sold. The beneficiary does not need to hold it for 12 months to qualify for the discount because that is measured from the deceased's acquisition date.

Of course, the more valuable the asset the more relevant the CGT discount becomes. This is also important if the Australian beneficiary has unused capital losses.

Other concerns when inheriting overseas property

The legal aspects relating to overseas property bequests can be tricky too, as shown in this reader's cautionary tale.

A READER'S TALE

My wife and I moved here from the United Kingdom. First my father died, then my mother, and the house was left to us — it was worth around $850,000 in Australian dollars. We knew nothing about the legal process and engaged a local lawyer, whom I plucked out of the phonebook. They told me they could handle an estate in the UK and quoted me fees of $5000 to do it.

They assured me there would be no need to engage an English solicitor to get probate. That was a mistake: everything had to be done by post, which added considerably to the time and the expense. Eventually, the process took over two years as certain documents got "lost". The sting in the tail was the fees went up to $50,000.

Mum had made specific bequests to grandchildren of $10,000 each but because of the delay in processing the estate, the estate ended up having to pay interest to the grandkids.

The lesson here, lawyer Kirsty Mackie says, is that the laws of inheritance vary widely throughout the world (even in Commonwealth countries) and it is advisable to engage a lawyer in the country where the assets are located, rather than engage an Australian lawyer who has no expertise in the relevant foreign law. That said, there are many excellent legal practitioners in Australia who are experienced in foreign law and it is worthwhile to ask the Law Society in your state or territory. However, the best suggestion would be to engage a local lawyer where those assets are located. In this case, it would have been better to engage a UK solicitor to deal with the UK property.

In relation to the interest, there is a general rule that interest is payable on any monetary bequest after one year from the date of death; however, as with most of the law, there are exceptions. The will could contain a specific instruction that interest is payable from a specific date, or if it relates to maintenance of a minor then the interest would be payable from the date of death. The rate of interest varies from state to state, and is subject to adjustment from time to time. Obviously the interest comes out of the estate, so it is wise to ensure that the estate is wound up efficiently.

The deceased's home

If the overseas property is the deceased's home, there are no main resident concessions unless it has been less than six years since the deceased was a resident of Australia for tax purposes. This means no two years to sell the property before any capital gains tax (CGT) is payable nor protection from CGT while it is occupied by a life tenant. In most cases the lack of main residence exemption on the deceased's overseas residence will not have much impact, because the CGT calculation still starts with the market value at DOD.

As long as the property in question is not located in Australia, the capital gain will be taxed under *Section 99B* like all other capital gains, so there are no offsetting capital losses nor any CGT discount.

Australian property owned by a non-resident

Australia has the right to tax Australian property even if it belonged to a non-resident, so the capital gains tax (CGT) calculation goes back to the purchase date. Since the deceased never qualified as an Australian resident for tax purposes, the property can't claim the main residence exemption. However, a small loophole exists: if the deceased died within six years of leaving Australia for tax reasons and had lived in the house, the executor might choose to apply the main residence concession. This essentially treats the property like their former home for tax purposes, reducing the potential CGT liability.

No tax will be payable on the gain up to DOD if the property is pre-CGT (20 September 1985). Upon death, the cost base is reset at market value.

The person who becomes liable for the tax on the sale of the Australian property depends on who owned the property when it was sold. Non-residents (i.e. the estate) are generally not entitled to the 50% CGT discount, though there are some concessions for properties acquired before 8 May 2012.

If it was still in the name of the estate when sold, the estate would have to pay tax in Australia on the capital gain, starting with the deceased's original purchase price, but then as the property had already been taxed in Australia, you as the Australian resident beneficiary could receive the sale proceeds free of tax.

If the property is transferred to you, the Australian resident beneficiary, before it is sold there is rollover relief — this means there is no CGT payable until you sell the property. When you sell the property you will be entitled to offset any capital losses you may have, and you may be able to use a portion of the CGT discount.

In the case of an Australian property acquired by the deceased after 19 September 1985, your cost base goes back to the deceased's cost base. When you sell the property you will effectively have to pay the deceased's CGT. When applying the CGT discount to this capital gain, you must consider the time it was owned by a non-resident after 8 May 2012 as not qualifying for the discount.

If the deceased acquired this Australian property before 19 September 1985, your cost base would be the market value at the date of death.

Receiving cash

The tax treatment for cash received depends on where it came from. If it was just money owned by the deceased when they died, there should be no tax consequences to receiving this money. Nevertheless, if it's over $10,000, it will raise a red flag with the ATO, who may ask for more details.

On the other hand, if that cash is the proceeds from the sale of an asset of the deceased's, any capital gain on that asset since DOD needs to be included in your tax return. If receiving cash from the sale proceeds of the estate selling an Australian property owned by the deceased, there should be no tax payable by the beneficiary because Australian tax should have already been paid by the estate. It is worth checking with the executor that the estate has completed an Australian tax return.

There is a big difference in how Australia taxes overseas estates compared with Australian resident estates. This, of course, leads to misunderstandings when it comes to cash sale proceeds received from overseas.

- In the case of Australian resident estates, you do not have to worry about the source of the cash unless it is the proceeds of a post-CGT asset in the same financial year as you become presently entitled.
- If you are a resident of Australia for tax purposes, Australia is entitled to tax your worldwide income, including distributions from trusts. Australia will be looking at the source of the cash you received. If that source was the sale of an asset, then regardless of how long ago (of course limited to sales after the deceased's death) your advisers will need to work out your share of the capital gain on that asset in accordance with Australian tax law, and pay the tax in Australia.
  - If listed shares are simply transferred into your name (i.e. left to you *in specie*) you start with a cost base of market value at DOD — that is the date when Australia began to have the right to tax any gain on those shares. When you do sell you will be entitled to

offset your capital losses and possibly to some CGT discount. The portion of discount is determined by the number of days the shares are owned by an Australian resident plus the number of days the shares are owned by a non-resident prior to 8 May 2012. So it is important that you know the day the deceased purchased the shares and any times they may have been a resident of Australia for tax purposes.

- It is not so simple when you receive sale proceeds from shares owned by the deceased at DOD, but sold by the estate before distributing the cash to you. *Section 99B* will treat the difference between the market value of the shares at DOD and the selling price as normal foreign income in your tax return. Therefore, there is no opportunity to offset your capital losses, or to apply any CGT discount. Even if you receive the sale proceeds in a different financial year to the estate selling, you still have to treat the gain as income.

Death benefits from a non-resident superannuation or pension fund

The tax treatment of these payments varies depending on how the deceased acquired the interest and the type of fund that is making the payment. There is no alternative if you receive a payment from a non-resident fund than to apply to the ATO for a ruling on your particular circumstances.

Foreign tax credits

If you end up paying tax in Australia on a distribution from a non-resident estate, you may be entitled to a foreign tax credit for any tax paid overseas by the estate on income or capital gains that is eventually distributed to you. But it must be a similar tax. For example, you are not entitled to a foreign tax credit for inheritance tax paid by the estate, but if the estate paid CGT and distributed the sale proceeds to you, you may be entitled to claim a foreign tax credit against any tax you have had to pay in Australia, if Australia has a double tax agreement with the country of which the estate is a resident.

What is the best option?

This is a complex area and obviously expert advice is important. If you are interested in trying to get the asset transferred to you, rather than have the estate sell it, seek legal advice regarding the will and whether this can actually be done. Make sure you don't contribute any money back into the estate to even out the distribution with the other heirs. If you make any contribution for the asset you receive, you are deemed to have purchased 100% of it off the estate for market value, which defeats the purpose. Though on the other hand, if you intend to hold the asset long term, actually buying the asset off the estate rather than inheriting it will give you a fresh start with the full 50% CGT discount.

It is important that you get all the information you need from the executor. There should be a document listing the value of the assets at DOD, but if you are receiving any assets *in specie* you will need to know when the deceased purchased them and the deceased's residency history during ownership. If there is taxable Australian property you will also need to know the date it was acquired by the deceased, the price they paid, plus any other items relevant to the cost base.

Depending on the competency of the executor, it may be necessary to obtain advice about the tax laws of the country of residence of the estate. This is best done through one of the big accountancy firms, such as BDO, which will have offices in that country to consult with.

Tax returns for deceased Australian residents and their estates

In many cases, the estate of the deceased will continue to earn income after death. This could be from investments such as dividends, trust distributions, interest and rent. Basically, income earned up to the date of death is included in the deceased's individual tax return. After that date, the income is included in a trust tax return for the estate. But regardless of which return the income is included in, it is the estate's responsibility to pay the tax. In the financial year of the deceased's death, both the DOD tax return and the estate tax return are entitled to the full tax-free threshold each, and to the normal stepped-up tax rates. For the first three financial years after date of death, the estate will be entitled to the tax-free threshold and stepped-up tax rates but will not have to pay a Medicare levy.

The deceased's individual date of death tax return should include:

- salary and wages earned up to DOD
- investment income up to DOD
- leave payments made before death
- capital gains or losses, where agreement to sell was made before death
- deductions incurred up to DOD
- accounting fees to prepare DOD tax return, even though these are incurred after death

- any taxable superannuation income received before death.

The estate's trust tax return should include:

- investment income received after death
- salary and wages received after death
- capital gains or losses on assets sold by the estate
- deductions for expenses incurred by the estate that relate to the earning of income.

Note that neither tax return includes accrued annual leave and long service leave payments made after DOD; these are not taxable. The treatment of superannuation received after death is covered in the superannuation chapter.

Income received after DOD in relation to an asset that the deceased owned with another person under a joint tenancy arrangement is generally treated as income of the surviving joint tenant and therefore not included in either the DOD or estate tax return.

Using capital losses before death

Capital gains are still taxable after death, but capital losses die with the deceased. Therefore, if possible, it is prudent to sell assets that carry unrealised capital gains to soak up any tax losses in the name of the person while they are still alive.

CASE STUDY

Bert had a substantial share portfolio. He had sold some shares, realising a $40,000 capital loss, and as there had been no capital gains to offset the loss he carried it forward in his tax return each year. When Bert's death was imminent, his accountant noticed some of the shares were now worth much more than Bert had paid — there was about $100,000 in unrealised capital gains.

These shares were sold, and the capital gain of $100,000 was reduced by the $40,000 capital losses. The remaining $60,000 was subject to the 50% discount. Notice how, in a quirk in the legislation, the 50% discount is calculated after the losses have been deducted.

As the principal ages, it is worthwhile considering whether to make gifts during their lifetime rather than after it. It's not just the principle of giving with a warm hand not a cold one — often the elderly person may have a lower income than the beneficiaries, and transferring assets before death could mean less tax on the capital gain.

If you are considering giving to a charity through your will, remember this will be considered a bequest, not a donation, so it will not qualify as a tax deduction for the estate. If you have sufficient taxable income, consider donating before you die.

CASE STUDY

Valerie is 93 and realises she has more than enough funds for the rest of her life. She wants to simplify her affairs by selling an investment property, which will trigger a $200,000 taxable capital gain. Her will includes a $200,000 bequest to the RSPCA. She realises that by donating the money from the sales proceeds now instead she can claim a tax deduction of $200,000, which will eliminate the CGT. If the estate sold the property and gave the bequest, it would not be allowed to offset the capital gain, because bequests are not tax-deductible.

Alternatively, inform your high-income heirs of your favourite charities, in case they want to donate something from their share of the estate and benefit from the tax deduction. Note this instruction cannot be given through the will, or it would be considered a bequest.

Remember that generally when an asset is transferred to a beneficiary, capital gains tax is not triggered: it rolls over, so that the beneficiary must pay the capital gains tax when they sell the asset, right back to the date the deceased acquired the asset. But in cases where Australia is likely to lose its taxing rights because the asset will be transferred *in specie* to a tax-advantaged beneficiary, the rollover does not apply and the capital gain up to date of death is taxed in the DOD tax return. This means that, while the beneficiary receiving the asset gets the inheritance you may have anticipated, the residual beneficiary will receive less, because the capital gains tax will be paid out of the estate, i.e. out of their share.

This problem arises when an asset is transferred to a beneficiary who was a non-resident at the date of the deceased's death and the asset is not taxable Australian property. It also arises when an asset is transferred to a superannuation fund or tax-exempt body, unless that exempt body is also a tax-deductible gift recipient.

Claimable deductions in the DOD return

All expenses incurred by the deceased prior to death — if they are allowable deductions — may be claimed in the DOD return. The kind of deductible expenses that apply here include work-related expenses such as tools and uniforms, professional subscriptions, rental expenses incurred in relation to an investment property and management fees paid to investment advisers. However, funeral expenses are not tax-deductible.

There are also special rules regarding depreciation, but these are somewhat complex and are a matter for discussion with your accountant.

Usually, in the first year or two after death, the estate pays tax on any income, but once beneficiaries become presently entitled they may be liable for the tax instead of the estate.

Present entitlement

"Presently entitled" means a person has a legal right to receive income or assets from a trust or estate in the present: the individual has an immediate and enforceable claim to the benefits, without any conditions or restrictions. Present entitlement grants the beneficiary control of the assets, including their distribution or use. This concept is crucial in determining the tax implications and timing of distributions within an estate plan. Understanding present entitlement enables effective structuring of estate plans to achieve the desired objectives.

It is unusual for any beneficiary to be presently entitled in the first year of the estate, because there is still so much uncertainty. In the first year, present entitlement would be signified by the actual distribution being received by the beneficiary before the end of the financial year. At the other end of the scale, in the final year of the estate the beneficiaries are regarded as fully presently entitled to all the income and capital gains of the estate for that year. If you only become presently entitled part-way through a year and want to separate the tax liability during the final year of the estate, it requires a full set of accounts to be drawn up during the year as well as at the end.

Remember, this is a simplified overview. For specific guidance on your situation, consult a qualified tax professional.

Action list

- ☐ Get your record keeping in order for your executor and beneficiaries.
  - See the appendix, Keeping the right records, on page 340.
  - I highly recommend the package of spreadsheets available to buy from: ***www.bantacs.com.au/shop-2/getting-your-affairs-in-order-made-simple/***
    They will guide you through the records you need for each type of asset and allow you to store a scanned copy of the relevant document beside each entry. As this record is totally digital, you can share it with everyone that needs to know — then there is no risk of losing information.
    Remember to type "Noel" into the voucher section of the shopping cart for a 20% discount.
- ☐ Review your will with the greater knowledge you have gained from this chapter to see if you need to explore making any changes.

5

Death and superannuation

Superannuation is a major asset in many estates, but many people don't realise that it is not automatically left in accordance with your will. This is because superannuation is not a personal asset, like property or shares that you own in your own name: it is held in trust for you by the trustee of your superannuation fund. When you die, your superannuation is classed as a trust asset not a personal asset, and therefore it is the trustee of your superannuation fund who has the final say in where your superannuation benefits will be paid.

If you are doing detailed estate planning yourself, you may want to remove or reduce the trustees' discretion, to help ensure your superannuation proceeds end up where you would like them to, using the various types of nominations available to you. If you have a self-managed superannuation fund (SMSF) the trust deed is a critically important document in determining how you can control payment of death benefits.

There are four important facts to consider when estate planning for your superannuation.

1. When a superannuation fund's member dies, their money has to be paid out of the fund.
2. Only certain people are eligible to receive a superannuation death benefit directly.
3. Insurance proceeds inside a superannuation fund may be heavily taxed on the member's death.
4. There can be a death tax on superannuation in some circumstances, and there are strategies to minimise this or avoid becoming eligible to pay it.

Key terms	Explanation
Member benefit	A payment made to a living member of a superannuation fund, such as a retiree. These are normally tax-free. A typical example is a payment to a member when they meet a condition of release such as retirement.
Death benefit	A payment made to an eligible beneficiary, after the death of a superannuation fund member. A death benefit may be taxable.
Transfer balance cap (TBC)	Limits the amount that can be converted to the retirement phase of super, which means a death benefit can only be retained in the superannuation environment if paid as a retirement income stream.
Death benefit nomination	This tells the trustee of your fund how to pay out your superannuation after your death. A ***non-binding nomination*** tells the trustee of your fund how you would like your superannuation to be paid out after your death, but the trustee does not have to follow it. A ***lapsing binding death benefit nomination*** is one that expires after a set time. Most non-self-managed super funds offer lapsing binding death benefit nominations that expire after three years.

Key terms	Explanation
Death benefit nomination *(continued)*	Providing a ***binding death benefit nomination*** (BDBN) is prepared correctly, the trustee of the super fund is legally obliged to do what it says when it comes to paying a death benefit. A ***non-lapsing binding death nomination*** is a binding death benefit nomination that does not expire — it continues indefinitely. A ***reversionary nomination*** is a special election that relates only to money that is in pension mode. It provides for the member's pension to be automatically continued ("reverted") to the person nominated. Whether or not it is legally binding on the trustee (like a binding death benefit nomination) will depend on the fund's trust deed.
Superannuation Industry Supervision (SIS) laws	The laws that, with the taxation laws, govern the treatment of death benefits from superannuation.
SIS dependant	A person classed as a dependant under superannuation legislation.
Tax dependant	A person classed as a dependant under tax legislation.

Key terms	Explanation
Concessional contribution	A contribution for which somebody, often the employer, has claimed a tax deduction. They are subject to an entry tax and form part of the taxable element of your super fund.
Non-concessional contribution	These are contributions for which nobody has claimed a tax deduction and include contributions from after-tax dollars and downsizing contributions. They are not subject to an entry tax and form part of the non-taxable component.
Taxable component	The portion of the super fund attributable to concessional contributions and fund earnings.
Non-taxable component	The portion of the super fund attributable to non-concessional contributions.
Legal personal representative (LPR) / Personal representative	A person who is legally authorised to represent a deceased individual and their estate. This term covers the executor/s or administrator of the estate.

Death benefits

Money can normally be left in superannuation as long as the member desires. However, once the member dies, the money has to be paid out of the fund, and this may be by an income stream, a lump sum, or a combination of the two.

There's also a time aspect — the ATO expects the superannuation death benefit to be paid as soon as practical, which they usually see as six months. Of course, this delay can be extended if there are mitigating circumstances.

The death benefits can be paid in cash, which may involve selling assets within the fund to fund the payment, or *in specie*, that is, by transfer of the assets themselves. This is a complex area, and expert financial advice is essential if you are considering *in specie* benefits.

A benefit payment made upon the death of a super fund member is called a super death benefit. Generally, the benefit can be paid to one or more of the person's dependants and/or to their legal personal representative (LPR), but the options and rules can be complicated. This is why it's sensible to get good advice to make sure the death benefit payment, and any proceeds from insurance inside super, go to your intended beneficiaries.

It's more complex for people with larger superannuation balances. For example, the transfer balance cap (TBC) limits the amount that can be converted to the retirement phase of super, and a death benefit can only be retained in the superannuation environment if paid as a retirement income stream. In some cases, the only strategies available are to commute some or all of the surviving member's existing pension back to the accumulation phase, or even cash out the death benefit itself. Alternatives such as testamentary trusts and investment options outside super may also need to be considered. Advice is essential.

Death benefit nominations

The big question is, how do you ensure that the people whom you would like to receive your superannuation actually get it? There are several options:

1. Do nothing and hope the trustee of your fund will do the right thing. This may be appropriate if your affairs are simple and there is no chance of a challenge to your estate.
2. Execute a non-binding nomination. This is a document which tells the trustee of your fund how you would like your superannuation to be paid. This does not bind the trustee, who still retains the discretion as to where your death benefits are to be paid. Usually, this nomination needs to be reviewed and renewed every three years, otherwise it lapses.
3. Execute a binding death benefit nomination (BDBN). Providing the nomination is prepared correctly, the trustee of the super fund is legally obliged to do what it says when it comes to paying a death benefit.

- A lapsing binding death benefit nomination is one that expires after three years. Most non-SMSFs offer lapsing binding death benefit nominations. To keep the nomination in place, it is necessary to review it every three years.
- A non-lapsing binding death nomination is one that does not expire — it continues indefinitely.

Any nomination may be updated or cancelled at any time to take into account changing circumstances. There may be a problem if the fund member has lost capacity, but subject to the rules of the fund, an enduring power of attorney (EPA) should be able to do what needs to be done. Just keep in mind that a binding nomination is invalid if all the requirements of executing it correctly, including witnessing requirements, have not been met.

Note that not all superannuation funds allow for BDBNs, and the rules may vary between funds. It's important to review any death benefit nominations regularly to reflect any changes in personal circumstances, such as the birth of a child or a relationship breakdown.

Disputes regarding BDBNs are on the rise, affecting both self-managed superannuation funds and retail funds. Common causes for these disputes include non-compliance with the super fund's trust deed terms and the mental capacity of the nominator at the time of making the nomination.

Recently, a BDBN was successfully contested by a family member who felt disadvantaged. Despite the nomination having been otherwise completed in accordance with the trust deed requirements, the deceased individual had failed to notify the second trustee of the trust, resulting in the conclusion that the nomination was not compliant with the trust's terms.

This case serves as one of many examples highlighting the utmost importance of strictly adhering to the trust's provisions when making a superannuation nomination for a self-managed super fund.

In Chapter 1, we discussed the concept of mental capacity extensively. With people living longer and often experiencing a decline in cognitive abilities late in life, capacity to make a BDBN is becoming an increasingly common source of dispute. In many instances, it may be advisable for the attorney to sign the nomination form instead of the fund member.

Eligible beneficiaries

Superannuation can pay benefits to the estate if directed to do so under a BDBN, or by the remaining trustees or the legal personal representative of the deceased. The super fund's trust deed may also influence the payment of death benefits.

Many people don't realise there are specific rules about who can receive superannuation death benefits. These are the spouse, children and financial dependants of the deceased person; also people who meet the criteria for an "inter-dependency" relationship with the deceased, as specified in superannuation laws.

Younger people often nominate their parents or siblings as beneficiaries, without realising that they are not eligible to receive the benefits from the fund. Parents and siblings are not eligible recipients unless they are also financial dependants. This is not usually the case. A superannuation fund therefore cannot usually pay death benefits directly to parents or siblings, even if they have been nominated as the recipients. Superannuation death benefits also can't be paid directly to charities, trusts or companies. To pay superannuation death benefits to someone other than an eligible recipient (including charities) you need to ensure your fund pays the death benefit to your estate. Then it will be distributed as directed by your will — and under your will you can nominate anyone you like to receive your superannuation death benefit.

In addition, if there is no eligible recipient nominated or located by the fund's trustee, the benefits will be paid to the deceased person's estate (their legal personal representative) and then distributed according to the terms of their will.

The only way a superannuation death benefit can be paid directly to anyone other than an eligible recipient is if there is no estate formed. This may happen in a situation where superannuation is the only asset of the deceased, or if their other assets are held as joint tenants and thus pass directly to the co-owner/s.

SIS-dependant and tax-dependant beneficiaries

There is a frequent misunderstanding about the application of "dependant" in superannuation law, particularly when paying death benefits. The definition of dependant in super law dictates who can receive death benefits; the definition in tax law determines if and how a recipient will be taxed.

Any of these eligible recipients for a person's superannuation death benefit may also be described as a "SIS dependant", to indicate that they meet the rules to be allowed to receive the benefit under super laws (SIS).

But there is a different definition of dependency when it comes to working out how they will be taxed on that death benefit. The main differences are that the definition of a "tax dependant" includes a former spouse and excludes children aged 18 years or over.

People who are classified as dependants for tax purposes are often called "tax dependants". The distinction is important because taxation rules are very different for dependants and non-dependants. In particular, tax dependants can generally receive superannuation benefits entirely tax-free, while non-dependants for tax purposes may pay quite substantial taxes on their inheritance.

So under SIS law, all children are dependants and therefore eligible to receive death benefits; but under tax law, adult children are not dependants, so they will pay tax on the taxable component of any death benefits they receive.

The estate

Superannuation proceeds may form part of an estate where a valid binding nomination is made in favour of the estate. The trustee may also require payments to an estate (in specific circumstances, e.g. if no valid binding nomination is in place), or exercise discretion to pay the death benefit to the estate.

Spouse

Your spouse includes another person (whether of the same or opposite sex) with whom you were in a relationship that was registered under a prescribed state or territory law, or who, although not legally married to you, lived with you on a genuine domestic basis in a relationship as a couple (a de facto spouse).

Child

This means any child of the deceased. It includes the deceased's natural, adopted and step-children, ex-nuptial (i.e. out of wedlock) children, their current spouse's children, and any child who was born through artificial conception procedures or under surrogacy arrangements with the member's current or then spouse.

Interestingly it doesn't include children of an individual's former spouse or a spouse who predeceased them, unless the children were adopted by the deceased.

Financial dependant

It is the super fund trustee's responsibility to decide whether any other person was financially dependent on the member at the time of death. The term "dependant" is not expressly defined in either super or tax legislation but has been considered by the courts on numerous occasions. The key principle is that it is not the value received from the member that establishes dependency, but the degree of dependency on that payment. This includes the extent to which the person relies on financial support provided by the other person to meet basic living expenses.

In a case where the grandparents paid school fees for their grandchildren it was decided that this did not establish financial dependency. This is because the parents had incurred the liability to pay fees and the payment was discretionary in nature and did not provide for the essential elements of life, such as food or shelter. To make it even more complex, a person could be deemed a financial dependant under SIS by a super trustee, but the ATO has determined that, in similar circumstances, no dependency existed.

Person in an interdependent relationship

An interdependency relationship between two people can be characterised by a close personal relationship, generally where the two people are living together, providing financial support, domestic support and personal care of a type and quality above the care and support normally provided by a friend or flatmate. It may also include a person who did not live with the deceased at the time of death but provided domestic support, financial support or personal care due to one or both of them having a physical, intellectual or psychiatric disability. They may be temporarily living apart due to one (or both) of them temporarily working overseas or serving a jail sentence.

Nominating a beneficiary

You are not required by law to nominate a beneficiary. If no beneficiary is nominated, the onus is on the appointed or remaining trustee/s of the fund to direct the proceeds of your super as they think fit. This may well be directly to your estate, or to other eligible beneficiaries who may come forward to make a claim, which could include children or partners from current or previous relationships.

This is a critical area to understand, as getting it wrong can be extremely costly. Your financial adviser should discuss estate planning with you in depth and help you prepare the appropriate documentation for your super fund.

A death benefit nomination could be reversionary for a pension, and binding or non-binding for all other super interests. Reversionary and binding nominations are only valid at the time of death if the person nominated is eligible to receive the benefit.

Reversionary nomination

A reversionary nomination can be made by people who are receiving a pension so that their pension automatically continues after their death ("reverts") to a single eligible beneficiary. The reversionary nomination, unlike a death benefit nomination, relates only to super money that is in pension mode.

This may be the best choice if the pensioner and beneficiary (most commonly a spouse) are certain they want the pension to continue being paid after death. If a reversionary nomination is in place, the beneficiary does not have to decide how they want to receive the money at a time of grief, and the funds will automatically be retained in the concessionally taxed superannuation environment. The surviving spouse has 12 months from date of death before the pension balance is included in their own transfer balance cap.

Not all SIS dependants are allowed to receive a deceased person's super as a pension. If the deceased was supporting someone financially, or in an interdependent relationship, that person may need to provide the super fund trustee with supporting documentation about the relationship, possibly by filling out a statutory declaration explaining the extent of the relationship.

Adult children are SIS dependants (who can receive their parent's superannuation directly from the fund) but they are generally not allowed to receive it as a pension once they turn 25. An income stream paid to a child under that age must cease once the child reaches 25, unless the child has a prescribed disability. At this point, the child must commute the income stream as a tax-free superannuation lump sum. So a reversionary nomination to a child can give them a terrific head start on their own superannuation — if they had instead received a lump sum, and their age made them ineligible to contribute to super, the money would have to stay outside the superannuation system.

Before age 25 they have a number of options, in line with those open to other eligible beneficiaries, including:

- taking the benefit as a single lump sum
- taking part of the benefit as a lump sum and the balance as an income stream.

If a member wishes to change a reversionary nomination after they have started their pension but before they have died, the process for doing so depends on the rules of their particular fund. Sometimes it might be necessary to stop the pension altogether and re-start it to make this change. It is worth getting advice before taking this step as it can have important tax and social security consequences.

While spouses nominating each other as the reversionary beneficiary of their income stream can be a good start in estate planning for superannuation, the reversionary nomination can only work for one of them. A back up plan is essential for dealing with death benefits once one of them passes and the survivor's reversionary nomination is no longer valid.

In this case, a BDBN can be useful as a cascading form of death benefit nomination. That is, a reversionary nomination would take effect first on the passing of one spouse, then the BDBN would be in place to deal with death benefits on the passing of the second spouse. Whether this is possible will depend on the trust deed: some have reversionary pensions prioritised over BDBNs; if it is the other way around, a BDBN to the estate would effectively overrule the reversionary pension.

Binding nomination

A binding death benefit nomination enables you to specify which SIS dependant/s you want to receive your super death benefit, and in what proportions, or to direct the super death benefit to your legal personal representative. Provided the binding nomination is valid, the trustees must pay a death benefit according to those instructions.

A valid binding nomination provides the most certainty that the death benefit will be paid according to your wishes. But a binding nomination may be more appropriate if the member wants any death benefit to be paid to the legal personal representative, or if they wish to nominate more than one dependant.

It's important to keep the nominations updated in line with changing circumstances. If the superannuation holder's circumstances or preferences change before their death, they can amend their binding nomination at any time, provided they have not lost capacity.

Non-binding death benefit nomination

A non-binding death benefit nomination enables you to indicate to the trustee who you would like to receive your super in the event of your death. It provides guidance for the trustee to decide which dependant/s should receive the death benefit; however, unlike binding nominations, the trustee has discretion when making the decision.

Non-binding nominations can be valuable where it is desirable to have flexibility at the time of death to determine how much is to be paid:

- to the estate, for example, to be placed into a testamentary trust
- as a lump sum to the estate to clear debts and to pay immediate expenses
- as a pension
- to multiple beneficiaries.

A non-binding nomination may also be appropriate where a beneficiary's circumstances are expected to change. For example, a child may have been a dependant for tax purposes when the estate planning was done, but at the time of your death you hope they may have become a non-dependant for tax purposes.

The downside is that the death benefit could be distributed in a manner that does not reflect your wishes.

Paying a death benefit to multiple beneficiaries

If the fund member wants their death benefit to be paid to multiple beneficiaries and makes a binding nomination, usually a fixed percentage of the death benefit is selected to be paid to each beneficiary. However, if these selections are not updated regularly, the outcome may not be what the testator desired. It may be preferable to use a non-binding nomination and allow the trustee to select how much of a death benefit is to be paid to each beneficiary at the time of death, with input from the fund member's financial adviser and solicitor.

CASE STUDY

Simon was a highly respected business executive who had three children from his first marriage. After the children had grown up and left home, he and his wife divorced, and sometime later he met and eventually married Yvonne, who had two children of her own. Simon's will left everything to his new wife, and included a clause that he wished his super to be included in the assets that were to go to her if he died. He died suddenly and, as required by law, the superannuation trustee wrote to all interested parties to see if they intended to claim on the estate. His three children, even though they were now highly successful in their careers, immediately lodged claims on the grounds that he had neglected them for his work when they were growing up.

The trustee disallowed these claims and decided to pay his superannuation to Yvonne. The three children appealed to the Superannuation Complaints Tribunal, a process that is available to anyone at no cost. I was Yvonne's financial adviser at the time, and her portfolio was frozen while the matter was being fought over. This meant we could not move assets to help her portfolio perform better. More than two years passed before the parties came to an agreement that required Yvonne to give Simon's three children from the first marriage almost one third of the estate. By now, she was a widow in her 70s and decided it was better to give in gracefully than spend the next five years fighting.

If Simon had inserted a binding nomination clause in his superannuation document, the direction would have been binding on the trustee, and his three children would have had less chance of a successful claim.

But a binding nomination is not always the right choice.

CASE STUDY

A wealthy couple attended an estate planning seminar I was giving and heard about the problems that can occur if there are potential squabbles in the family and a binding nomination has not been put in place. When the seminar finished, they went home, called their financial adviser and instructed that a binding nomination be prepared whereby they left half of their superannuation to the surviving spouse on the death of either one of them, with the balance to be divided equally between their two children. This was a happy family, and the children were both high-earning professionals who got on well.

About six months later he died suddenly, leaving around $2 million in superannuation. If there had been no binding nomination, the trustee could have paid the entire $2 million to the spouse tax-free and she could have gifted any amount she wished to either of their children tax-free. However, the binding nomination forced the trustee to pay $1 million to the wife and $500,000 each to the two children. Because of their tax brackets, this resulted in a total tax bill of $170,000.

There are a couple of lessons here. First, a binding nomination is like a strong drug — great if you apply it in the right way, but potentially dangerous. In this case, they acted without getting advice suited to their particular circumstances, and misunderstood the likely tax consequences of payments to their high-earning children. Second, no one has a crystal ball — if he had died at a different time, it might have been advantageous to allow the trustee of his superannuation to pay some of the death benefit to the estate to go into a testamentary trust for his family's benefit.

Life insurance in super

It is a common strategy to arrange your life insurance through your super fund. The fund can often buy insurance at wholesale rates, and by using salary sacrifice you can effectively pay the premiums from pre-tax dollars. However, depending on who receives them, the proceeds may be taxable when you die.

Whether your life insurance payout is taxable in Australia generally depends on your policy ownership structure: inside or outside of super.

- If your life insurance is in your super fund, the proceeds (as with the rest of your super) will be paid out as a "superannuation death benefit" to your permitted beneficiaries. Only some beneficiaries can receive your death benefit from super tax-free.
- If the policy is held outside superannuation, a life insurance benefit paid directly to your spouse or child is generally not subject to taxation. If there are no nominated beneficiaries on your policy, the death benefit is usually paid into your estate and will then typically be distributed by the executor as part of the estate via your will.

If your super is paid to someone who is not classified as a tax dependant, having insurance included in the benefit can make a big difference to the tax they pay if you die before turning 65 and your super fund claimed a tax deduction for the insurance premiums. That's because your whole super death benefit, including the insurance, will be divided into several parts — one of which will be taxed at up to 30% (plus Medicare if applicable) rather than the normal rate of up to 15% (plus Medicare if applicable).

CASE STUDY

Robin started his super account at age 20. At 26, when he had around $10,000 super built up from employer contributions and $290,000 of death cover, he was tragically killed in a car accident and, as he had no dependants, his total death benefit of $300,000 was to be paid to his parents via the estate.

If Robin had lived until 65, he would have had super for 45 years (from age 20 up to 65). He only completed six of those 45 years and so 6/45ths of his death benefit ($40,000) would be taxed at the usual rate of up to 15%. The other 39/45ths ($260,000) would be taxed at up to 30%. The total tax paid by the estate could be up to $84,000. (At least there is no Medicare levy payable by the estate.)

If Robin hadn't had any insurance, the benefit would have been a lot lower (only $10,000) but the whole amount would be taxed at up to 15%. In this case, at least the parents were still better off thanks to the insurance. But it could have been very different if Robin had already built up quite a bit of super and didn't have much insurance.

This special extra tax rate of up to 30% doesn't apply for people who die after reaching 65, even if they have insurance and even if it is paid to beneficiaries who are not dependants.

Typically, adult financially independent children are classified as non-dependants for this purpose. The same is normally true for parents (relevant for very young people who have life insurance in super).

On the other hand, a spouse or child who is still dependent will be classified as a tax dependant and no tax will be paid if the death benefit is paid as a lump sum, even if the death benefit includes insurance.

As the following example shows, it can be a complex process with unintended consequences. Keep in mind that where tax is payable by an estate the tax becomes a general liability of the estate. Things can get complicated if the deceased is older and the estate does not have the money to pay the tax.

CASE STUDY

Greg is a single father aged 50 with three adult children who all work. One of them lives at home with him. His house was worth $380,000 in 2008 when his will was drafted. He has $300,000 in super fund A and $15,000 in super fund B. There is also a $300,000 insurance policy in super fund B — this is the fund that is paying the premiums.

He wanted his will to treat his children equally. Therefore, it was drafted to give Lara, the eldest, the proceeds of Fund A, Damien the proceeds of Fund B and the residue of his estate to Alex, who was living at home. Greg figured that would be the house and the contents.

He gave his two super funds a binding death benefit nomination to make sure his death benefits from each fund went to his estate and would be distributed in accordance with his will.

Unfortunately, the will drafter didn't understand the effect of the death tax on insurance policies held in superannuation. When Greg died suddenly, the children got a second terrible shock when they discovered they were not going to be treated equally at all.

Super funds do not deduct the death tax and send the balance to the estate. Instead, they send the entire amount to the estate, and it is the estate that has the obligation to send the death tax to the ATO. Because the will specifically gave "the proceeds of Fund A" to Lara and "the proceeds of Fund B" to Damien, they are entitled to the whole of $300,000 and $315,000 respectively. The tax still has to be paid, but it won't be coming out of the proceeds received from either of Fund A or Fund B. Greg's executor is responsible for paying $45,000 death tax on the benefit from Fund A and even more on the Fund B death benefit (remember this fund had insurance and so part of the death benefit will be taxed at up to 30%).

Because Lara and Damien have received specific bequests, the tax can only be paid out of the residue of the estate. Using a concept known as "marshalling", the executor will probably have to sell the home to pay the tax bill, leaving Alex with much lower net benefits. Not only has Alex borne the cost of the tax payable on both of the superannuation payouts, they have also lost the family home to pay the tax bill.

If the two super fund lump sum death benefits had been paid directly to Lara and Damien, they would at least have been responsible for their own tax (rather than it all falling on Alex). But it still wouldn't have achieved what their father wanted (roughly equal treatment for all of them), because much more tax would be paid on the benefit going to Damien than the same amount being paid to Lara.

It is critical that anyone drafting a will understands that all assets are not treated equally for tax purposes. The difference between CGT-free assets like the family home and investment properties that carry a CGT liability are generally well known, but few people seem to understand the tax treatment of insurance policies held within superannuation, let alone the different tax treatment of the various components arising from contributions made to superannuation funds. As the above example shows, failure to take this tax into account can have distressing and unforeseen consequences.

It's worth also bearing in mind that if superannuation death benefits are paid directly to any of the children (rather than via the estate) it becomes part of their taxable income.

While tax offsets make sure they don't pay any more tax than the rates discussed earlier, this might still impact their eligibility for things that depend on their taxable income (certain government benefits, the tax rate they pay on their own employer super contributions, etc).

The death tax

Whenever I make a speech to retirees, I talk about the death tax of 15% (or 17% when it includes the Medicare levy), which can apply to superannuation death benefits. Most people have never heard of it and believe that Australia doesn't have death duties. While it is not, strictly speaking, a "death duty" the effect is the same. So take the time to get your head around it — it's an easy tax to minimise with a bit of planning.

Member superannuation benefits (payments to the member from their own super during their lifetime) are tax-free as long as the member is over 60, but the death tax applies to any taxable portion of your superannuation fund that is given to a person who is not a tax dependant. A spouse is always a tax dependant, whether they have a separate income or not, but adult children who are financially independent are classified as non-dependants for tax purposes.

The tax is only paid on the taxable component of the benefit, which is the money contributed as concessional contributions, along with the fund's earnings; the tax-free component is the non-concessional contributions.

So, if the tax does apply, how is it calculated?

If the payment is made directly to a beneficiary (rather than to the estate), it is taxed at a maximum of 17%, not a flat 17%. The tax is deducted by your superannuation fund before paying your beneficiary the death benefit. The tax paid is recorded on a PAYG payment summary (similar to wages); when your beneficiary lodges their personal tax return, the assessable amount received and PAYG withheld must be reported. If they have a high income, or if the sum is large, the tax is rebated so that no more than 17% is payable. If the beneficiary has a low income, they may even receive a refund of the tax paid by your super fund.

If the deceased was under 65 at the time they died, some of the taxable component can be taxed at an even higher rate: up to 32% with the Medicare levy.

If the death benefit is paid to the estate, no tax is deducted by the super fund — it will be taxed based on who gets the money. It is left up to the executor of the estate to work out any tax payable and remit PAYG to the tax office. If the estate ultimately distributes the benefit to a non–tax-dependant, it must be paid net of tax. Because estates don't pay the Medicare levy, the rate is slightly lower (15% instead of 17%).

One way to reduce the death tax is by way of a cash-out and recontribution strategy. This involves making tax-free withdrawals from your fund once you have turned 60, and — provided you are still eligible to contribute to superannuation — recontributing the money back to the fund. Because this recontribution comes from after-tax dollars, there is no entry tax, and it stays exclusively in the tax-free component of the fund.

CASE STUDY

Les and Ivy are in their late 60s. He has $900,000 in superannuation and she has no super. When they checked with the fund on the break-up of the components, they discovered it consisted of $700,000 taxable and $200,000 non-taxable. After consultation with their financial adviser, Les withdrew $660,000 from his fund and then recontributed $330,000 as a non-concessional contribution using the three-year bring-forward rule. He contributed $330,000 to a new super fund for

Ivy, as a non-concessional contribution. There is no entry tax on non-concessional contributions.

Let's look at the balances of the super funds before and after the transactions. Just bear in mind that you cannot choose which component you withdraw from — the withdrawal will be split in the percentage of the existing balances.

Before the withdrawal, Les' balance was 78% taxable and 22% tax-free. Therefore, the withdrawal of $660,000 will be split in those proportions. Les' withdrawal will be $515,000 taxable and $145,000 tax-free. His remaining balance will be reduced to $240,000 and the components will become $185,000 taxable and $55,000 tax-free.

The recontribution of $330,000 into his own fund will all go to the tax-free area because it's a non-concessional contribution, so his balance will be $570,000, made up of $385,000 tax-free and $185,000 taxable. The withdrawal and recontribution strategy has reduced his taxable component from $700,000 to just $185,000. Ivy's balance will initially be all tax-free.

Note that all earnings on the balance of both funds will be added to the taxable component, so as time passes, the taxable component will gradually increase in both funds. But keep in mind that we can now contribute to superannuation to

> age 75 without passing the work test, as long as the fund balance as at 30 June of the previous financial year is less than $1.9 million. The recontribution strategy can be repeated after three years and further reduce the taxable component.

It's important to seek advice before using these strategies, because there could be estate planning issues. The bring-forward rule can also be a bit complex and has the potential to create a penalty if not used properly. However, it has the potential to save tens of thousands of dollars in death tax. It's certainly worth investigating.

Many retirees are in pension phase, which means the earnings on their fund are tax-free, as are the withdrawals if they are aged 60 or over. However, the tax-free status of the fund does not mean that all the components become tax-free as well. There will almost certainly still be taxable and non-taxable portions of the components, with the death tax applying to the taxable component when paid to a non-dependant.

A reader asked if the death tax could be avoided by leaving the money to a charity. There is no joy here, as a charity is treated in the same way as a non-dependant. A much better option for anybody who wants to leave money to charity would be to withdraw it from superannuation before they die, make an immediate donation and claim a tax deduction.

However, if you are receiving Centrelink benefits, take advice before doing this, because a gift of more than $10,000 could be regarded as a deprived asset.

If you are considering a binding nomination, make sure you clearly understand the implications before setting it up. Once a valid binding nomination is in place, the trustee may lose the discretion to distribute the proceeds of the deceased's superannuation fund in the most tax-effective manner.

A simple way out of the death tax is for the fund member to cash in the entire superannuation balance at a time of their choosing and invest it outside the superannuation system. Alternatively, take advice about giving a trusted friend or relation an enduring power of attorney (EPA) that includes a clause expressly authorising conflict transactions. Then, if death appears imminent, the attorney could withdraw the entire superannuation balance tax-free and deposit it in the member's bank account. Remember, if you are considering this strategy, that an attorney cannot do anything to benefit themselves unless there is a conflict clause in the power of attorney document. Given that the attorney may well be a possible recipient of the superannuation proceeds, a conflict clause is essential. This is a matter for expert legal advice.

Often, for smaller balances, the tax advantages of superannuation are negligible, so in some cases closing your pension or superannuation account and investing in your own name is the simplest way to avoid such taxes.

Another strategy is to withdraw all your superannuation tax-free before you die. I appreciate that the date of one's death is a hard one to pick, but remember that superannuation is nothing more than an investment structure that lets you hold assets in a low tax or zero tax environment. For most people, there will come a time when the potential 17% tax on death is much greater than any tax savings that could be generated by holding the money inside superannuation.

CASE STUDY

Janet, aged 80, is a widow with no tax dependants whose main asset is $400,000 in superannuation. If she died, there could be a death tax of up to $68,000 deducted from the superannuation proceeds. However, if she withdrew the entire $400,000 and invested it outside the superannuation system, the tax on the income from it should be zero, as she would qualify for the tax offsets we mentioned previously, and the money would not be subject to the death tax. Just taking action at the right time would save the estate almost $70,000. If the beneficiaries of Janet's estate are her adult, financially independent children (non-dependants for tax purposes), she may see this as an excellent protection, even if she has a healthy fund balance and it ends up costing her a little more in tax personally.

Contributing to a fund in pension mode

Once an income stream is commenced, that account can no longer be contributed to. However, having an income stream does not mean further contributions cannot be made for or by an individual into superannuation. Such contributions will be made to the accumulation account of the member and once a condition of release is satisfied on the accumulation account, it can be used to commence a new income stream account or accessed by way of a lump sum.

It is worth remembering that at the time an individual commences an income stream, they may also face restrictions on their ability to make further contributions into superannuation, which could include age-based restrictions and/or passing a work test.

Self-managed super funds

Self-managed super funds (SMSFs) need special attention when estate planning is being done. Usually the trustees of the fund are the members, often a couple, and a major issue is who would act as trustee if one or more of them became incapacitated. I have long recommended that the trustee of any SMSF be a company, which is able to appoint a replacement director if one of the directors become legally incompetent due to a disability. Another option would be for the trustee to give an enduring power of attorney to another person who could take over when they are unable to act. There is also the issue of the assets in the fund. Are they liquid assets such as listed shares, or are they non-liquid assets such as business premises? Is it important to the family to retain those assets inside super if a fund member dies? Are the fund assets structured to be able to pay a death benefit in the event of the death of one of the members?

For starters let's just focus on one issue — the trustee. The choice is for the members of the fund to be trustees, or for the fund to appoint a company as trustee. Even though anybody who is well advised, and who takes that advice, will have a company as trustee, around 34% of SMSFs have individual trustees — the members. In this case, generally every trustee must be a member of the fund and every member of the fund must be a trustee.

So far so good, but think about what would happen if a member became incapacitated. An incapacitated person cannot act as trustee, which means they would be forced to exit the fund unless they had given an EPA to somebody else who did have the capacity to act for them.

If the fund happened to be a single member fund with a corporate trustee, and the sole member and sole director of the company becomes incapacitated, the fund would have to be wound up unless an EPA had been given to someone else to act on the sole member's behalf.

Many SMSFs have been formed to borrow for residential real estate. Imagine what would happen if a fund member became incapacitated, no power of attorney was in place, and the fund had to quickly find the money to pay out the member who had to leave the fund.

Another issue is that trustees are personally liable for the liabilities of the fund. "That's not a big issue," I hear you say, a superannuation fund is only a vehicle that holds assets — how could it possibly have a liability! Let's look at some case studies, one quite extreme and the other quite commonplace.

CASE STUDY

Consider a recent action by the tax office against a couple I'll call Mr and Mrs X. They were Egyptians living in Australia, and were the trustees of their own fund.

After a family dispute, Mr X withdrew all the money in the fund and departed with it to take up permanent residence in Egypt. Mrs X found herself trustee of a fund that no longer had any assets. Because Mr X had not satisfied a condition of release, the ATO took the view that there had been wrongful withdrawal from the fund and took away its concessional tax status.

The result was a tax bill, to the fund, of over $900,000. Given that Mr X had taken the money, Mrs X was naturally outraged, and she chose to fight the ATO in court. When the litigation ended, and the court found in favour of the tax office, the SMSF, of which Mrs X was the only trustee likely to be held to account, owed over $2 million when the penalties and court costs were taken into account. If the trustee had been a shelf company, her liability may have been minimal.

CASE STUDY

Mr and Mrs Smith have their own fund, with themselves as trustees. The fund owns an investment property, and one day somebody is injured on the property. It turns out that there was no adequate insurance over the property. As the trustees, Mr and Mrs Smith could be personally liable, and if the fund could not meet the costs their personal assets could be at risk.

The message is clear — if you have an SMSF, get yourself a corporate trustee, and make sure enduring powers of attorney are in place for all members. The cost is small compared to the potential liability.

Action list

- ☐ Decide whether it will work best to leave the trustee full discretion to distribute your super, or whether to make any kind of nomination for your benefits.
- ☐ Review any existing insurance within super. Ensure your family and executor/s know of its existence.
- ☐ Take a look at the taxable and non-taxable components in your superannuation, and see if there are ways you can increase the non-taxable proportion.
- ☐ If you have an SMSF, check your trustee situation, and get advice on whether to make any changes.

6

Rounding off your estate planning

If life is "like a box of chocolates", so is estate planning. In this chapter we cover an assortment of issues that may be relevant to you, but which didn't fit neatly into the chapters so far — issues that are neither specifically legal, tax-related nor superannuation-related. These include:

- how changes in your family structure — new relationships, marriage, separation and divorce — may affect your estate planning
- avoiding the credit card trap our banking system sets up for seniors, especially widows
- Centrelink issues for couples — particularly relevant to your wills

- how your choices about funding residential aged care may affect your estate planning
- using investment bonds for estate planning
- equity release as a source of funds, and its effects for your beneficiaries
- granny flat pros and cons — for family dynamics, Centrelink, CGT, and your will
- leaving your digital assets in good hands
- organising and funding your funeral.

Changes in your family structure

New relationships, marriage, new children, separation, and divorce — major life events have far-reaching implications. Whilst family law is a Commonwealth jurisdiction, how marriage and divorce is dealt with in a will or EPA can be different from state to state and you must consult your solicitor to clarify the position in your state or territory. Failing to recognise and respond to these events appropriately can lead to unintended — and potentially unfavourable — outcomes. This is why it's important to review your estate planning whenever these big life events happen. You cannot afford to procrastinate.

- Reviewing and updating your will is one of the most important things you can do for those you care about.
- Reviewing and updating your financial EPA, and its health and lifestyle equivalent, is one of the most important things you can do for yourself and for your loved ones.

These are not times to put forward planning and estate planning in the too-hard basket; a comprehensive review of your legal documents is necessary. These documents distribute power, wealth and control — areas that are ripe for conflict. I'm sure you want to lessen the risk of unintentional and undesirable outcomes.

A common case of problems with a will might be where a couple separate, but do not divorce. He re-partners and forms a de facto relationship with another woman, but never changes his will. As time goes by, he ends up with two children from the first marriage and one to his de facto. Both women detest each other. He's also estranged from the children of his first marriage. Imagine the minefield that would be left behind if he passes without first updating his will.

Protecting assets in new relationships

As life expectancies increase, it's becoming more common for mature people to start a new relationship later in life. Usually this happens after a partner dies or when there's a divorce. Both people involved may have children from previous relationships, and there well may be substantial assets involved.

There is usually a consensus between the couple that certain assets will become joint assets, while other assets are to be quarantined to make sure they eventually go to the children of the partner who brought these assets into the relationship. There are several strategies to ensure this happens, but the fundamental choice is whether it is achieved by documentation, or by holding the assets in the name of a person or entity where they can't be available to the other party's relations on death.

If the couple buy a property to live in, they may want to buy it as tenants in common, rather than joint tenants. This means that they each have a discrete share of the property, which can be willed to their individual estates, whereas assets held as joint tenants pass automatically to the survivor upon death of the other partner, irrespective of the terms of any will.

CASE STUDY

Doug and Margie bought a property for $1 million when they were ready to move in together. Because their assets were unequal, Margie contributed $600,000 to the purchase price and Doug contributed $400,000. To keep the money separate, they bought the property as tenants in common, with Margie owning six-tenths and Doug owning only four-tenths.

Another strategy would have been to execute a binding nomination to the trustee of their superannuation fund, instructing them to transfer the proceeds on death to specific people in certain proportions. Nominations can only be made to "dependants" such as spouses or children.

A further option may be to hold the assets in a family trust, but this is a more complicated way to proceed. While it may be effective at protecting them from creditors in some cases, money in a family trust is still up for grabs if there is a relationship dispute. Furthermore, if the family residence is owned by a trust, it loses the primary residence CGT exemption.

Binding financial agreements

It's a fact of life that not every relationship lasts the distance, and when couples live together for a specified minimum period, or longer, they acquire rights over certain individual and jointly owned assets in the event of a separation. Good preparation from the start tends to save a lot of problems down the track.

A great idea for both parties is to execute a binding financial agreement (BFA) under the *Family Law Act 1975 (Cth)*, which sets out what will happen to both parties' assets if the relationship ends. A BFA can also assist to manage inheritances coming to the individuals.

BFAs are most useful for couples with children from earlier relationships, or with significantly different assets, expectations, or responsibilities to a family company or trust. They can protect both parties in a relationship — saving a lot of money in mediation and legal fees if a break-up happens by determining in advance what should happen to the assets.

It's an awkward topic to raise in many cases, but probably the best time to do it is when you are making wills — this should happen early in any relationship that is intended to be permanent. The wills set out in writing the wishes of each partner in relation to their assets if one of them dies, and the BFA sets out their wishes if they split up. It's much easier to do it when you think you won't need it, rather than waiting until the relationship is looking rocky.

BFAs can be made before a relationship starts, during a relationship, or after a relationship has broken down. They can be expensive documents to prepare, as they are not subject to the scrutiny of the court and there are detailed obligations on the solicitor to provide extensive legal advice on the advantages and disadvantages of the agreement. The other party is also required to obtain independent legal advice on the agreement for it to be binding. However, a BFA can never be made completely watertight; they always remain open to dispute.

CASE STUDY

Cecil and Doris met in their early 60s. He was a widower and she had been divorced a few years before. I have seen the BFA they signed before they started to live together, and it is a very tightly drawn-up document. It listed their individual assets in detail and clearly stated that on the death of one of them, or if their relationship broke down, each of them would have the assets as disclosed in the agreement. They never married, but lived in a de facto relationship for more than 15 years. During all this time, they went to great lengths to keep their finances separate. To all intents and purposes, they were a devoted couple, and in the last few years of Doris' life when she became quite ill, Cecil was the perfect, dutiful partner and took great care of her.

Eventually Doris died and life appeared to proceed normally. Then, exactly six months from the date of her death, her children were flabbergasted to receive a letter from Cecil's solicitors to tell them he had commenced a claim on the estate. My solicitor told me that anyone in that position is entitled to make such a claim; however, he did say that the BFA would have great weight during the mediation process and possible court action that was almost certain to happen.

The lesson here is to never take anything for granted. A situation that appears to be all rosy can change overnight.

It is essential to have any BFA drawn up by a solicitor. For the agreement to be binding, both parties must have obtained independent legal advice, and statements to this effect must be attached to the agreement. This prevents either party claiming that they did not understand what they were signing. A further essential element is that the information provided by both parties is honest and no assets are omitted. If you forget to mention the unit in Port Douglas due to a memory lapse, you might find that your agreement is later set aside by a court.

For example, a couple might be happy to share all their assets in accordance with the *Family Law Act* in the event of a split, except the beach house that has been in one family for generations. It is still best to have the BFA list all assets, for clarity.

While there is a general perception that BFAs are designed to protect the assets of wealthy people, it is also common for people to use them for emotional reasons.

CASE STUDY

Andrew sold his business for a huge sum, went through a divorce then started a new relationship with the woman of his dreams. He was too much in love to worry about a BFA but she insisted on it. Her reasoning? So that none of their friends or family could claim that she had married him for his money.

What if you don't have a BFA? It is possible to make one at any time during a relationship, including after marriage, and that is a better option than leaving decisions to the uncertainties and delays of the Family Court. A well-thought-out agreement can eliminate an area of possible tension and leave both parties free to concentrate on their relationship. After all, that's what marriage is supposed to be about.

If you are planning to marry, don't leave discussion of a financial agreement until just before the wedding — a last-minute rush could easily give rise later to questions of duress. As one Californian family lawyer put it: "Pre-nups shouldn't be signed within earshot of the church wedding bells."

It is wise to draft your BFA and will at the same time to make sure that the clauses in the will and the provisions in the financial agreement align. A BFA is a useful tool, but things can go amiss if one of the parties dies or lose capacity. This is why wills and enduring powers of attorney should be carefully drawn up to cover these situations if they occur. This is a job for an expert estate lawyer.

Marriage

How marriage (and divorce) is dealt with in a will or EPA differs from state to state — you must consult your solicitor to clarify the position in your state or territory. In all jurisdictions, if you marry after your will has been made, your will is revoked by the marriage. In most (but not all) jurisdictions, if the will explicitly states that it has been made in contemplation of marriage, the will is not revoked. Divorce revokes all or part of the will unless there is specific wording to counteract this.

However, some aspects of your will can endure after marriage, even if you have not updated it. Specifically, if your earlier will contained provisions that relate to your new spouse, such as gifts to them, or designating them as an executor or trustee, these clauses will persist once you have married.

Upon marriage, the appointment in your EPA of any person other than your new spouse is revoked. Unlike a will, there is no precedent for making an EPA in contemplation of marriage. In any case, you will want to ensure that any other attorneys are able to work well with your spouse, should the EPA become effective.

Separation

Unlike marriage, separation does not carry immediate legal consequences for your will. However, it should serve as a powerful trigger to review it. Separation also has no automatic effect on an EPA granted to your now-ex-spouse.

This can be a traumatic time, but it's essential that you take advice and revisit your will in keeping with your changing circumstances. When separating, you will be making crucial decisions about arrangements, the division of matrimonial property, and the care of your children, if applicable.

If you procrastinate and never get around to redoing your will, your estranged partner may end up inheriting the bulk of your assets, as per your original will. Moreover, if your estranged spouse is appointed as your executor, they could assume that role upon your death, which might be far from your preferred outcome, given the relationship breakdown.

Divorce

Divorce introduces a whole different set of dynamics when it comes to your will, distinct from both marriage and separation. In most states and territories, gifts to your former spouse or their appointment as executor and trustee within a will are revoked.

If you still want them to be effective, you can — in some states and territories — include within your will a "contrary intention" clause, which states that the gift or appointment is still to take effect despite the divorce. However, it must be stressed that each state and territory has different legislation for how it deals with the effect of divorce on a will, and it is vital that you check with your solicitor whether a contrary intention clause can be used.

Whatever your intentions, it remains crucial to prepare a new will after divorce. This ensures that your testamentary intentions are clear, especially concerning former spouses and other beneficiaries. The financial and property adjustments commonly associated with divorce often necessitate a comprehensive review of your will — good legal advice is essential.

Bizarrely, the same is not true of an EPA — at least, not in most states. In Queensland and the ACT, divorce revokes an EPA to an ex-spouse. In all other states, the EPA must be revoked to remove it from a divorced partner, and if the principal has lost capacity to make their own decisions their EPA cannot be altered.

The credit card trap

A major goal of estate planning is to make life easy for the people left behind when you die. One of the most overlooked traps is lack of access to a credit card for a widow or widower.

Credit cards for retirees has been a hot topic for years. Everybody has a credit card when working, but when they retire the situation changes. Possibly they had a corporate card that was cancelled when they resigned, or as often happens, the family has a principal card held in the name of one partner, with the spouse having a supplementary card that is subservient to the principal card.

Then retirement comes and the corporate card is no longer available — or a partner dies and the survivor is unable to get a credit card of their own. Time and time again I've heard of people who were long-time customers of their bank, had a perfect credit record and substantial assets, and who were still refused a credit card.

Supplementary credit cards have other problems too. Many families have one main credit card, with the partner and other family members using supplementary cards, which keeps fees down. Unfortunately, with most such cards, as soon as one of the cards becomes lost or stolen all associated cards are blocked. This can be particularly embarrassing if you're travelling overseas.

Obviously, the solution is for couples to have individual credit cards, but as an email from a reader pointed out, it is difficult for retirees to qualify for a credit card.

A READER'S TALE

My husband and I have had a 40-year association with a major bank, have paid off numerous loans and have a history of never missing a payment. We are 62 and 73, and are self-funded retirees with substantial assets. After reading your articles I decided to apply for a credit card in my own name, which has to be done online. It was

> declined by the bank's computer on the grounds that I had no taxable income. I can't see the logic of this, and am concerned that my 40 years' loyalty with the bank appears to count for nothing. The bank's decision makes me feel discriminated against both as a married woman and a grandmother. Do you have any ideas how I can overcome this absurdity?

Another reader emailed me to say that the Coles Mastercard was freely available to everybody and it was wrong to suggest otherwise. I did some checking on that card and discovered it's an NAB card administered through Citibank. In the interests of research I decided to apply for the Coles Mastercard but was pessimistic about the outcome because a direct application to Citibank by myself two years earlier had been knocked back in a matter of hours.

When I was a banker many years ago, the criteria for lending were based on the 3C's: character, capacity, and collateral. Times have changed — the modern online credit card application ignores collateral (at no stage are you asked to list your assets) and character must be based solely on your credit score. You are asked to give a total of your household expenses, but there is no place to provide them in detail. Now it seems to be just a box-ticking exercise based solely on what they regard as your capacity to pay. You are required to produce evidence of income, and a copy of your latest payslip is specifically mentioned. This obviously presents a problem for retirees because most don't work and therefore cannot produce a payslip. However, NAB assured me that superannuation income is taken into account when you are proving capacity to repay the loan. As proof of income, I included a statement from my superannuation fund, giving the superannuation balances of my wife and myself, accompanied by a statement from the fund as to my expected income from pensions.

I must give Citibank their due: I had numerous phone calls from friendly staff, all based in the Philippines, but they were mainly concerned with ticking boxes. I mentioned to them that I have had a Virgin credit card for 20 years run by Citibank and looking at the transactions could give them a very good idea what kind of payer I was.

But the upshot was I did get approved for the Coles Mastercard, with the rather unusual limit of $13,600. And age was not a problem — I am now well past retirement age.

So, one option for older people who have been knocked back for other credit cards is to have a go at applying for the Coles No Annual Fee Platinum Mastercard. As there are no fees, there's nothing to lose. But there is no guarantee of success. I mentioned the Coles card in my newsletter and many readers applied for it. Some were approved and some declined — there seemed to be no logic to the different decisions.

Getting a card, as a retiree who has recently lost their partner, can be really hard. A much better option is for each partner to acquire a credit card in their own name before the main breadwinner finishes work, when it would be much easier to obtain it. This could prevent much heartache later. One last possible solution is for one of your adult children to get a credit card and make you a supplementary card holder.

The fallback position is a debit card. You don't have to qualify because all you are doing is spending your own money. A good debit card can do almost everything credit cards can do, except they don't give you reward points. But in my experience, most reward points are fairly worthless, so I wouldn't waste my decisions on any points I might get.

Unfortunately, it's all much more difficult than it needs to be. Just don't keep putting it off — it's much easier to get a credit card before you retire.

Centrelink issues for couples

The majority of retirees are on some form of income support, and estate planning should consider how best to keep this going when a partner dies. The age pension is calculated on both an assets and an income test, and the test that produces the lowest pension is the one used. But the rates of pension payable vary between homeowners and non-homeowners and couples and singles. You can download the appropriate pension charts from my website, ***www.noelwhittaker.com.au***, under Resources, and run various scenarios using my ***Age Pension Calculator*** and ***Deeming Calculator***.

The most important thing to note is the difference between the assets cut-off point for a single person and that for a couple. At date of writing, the cut-off point for a single homeowner was $667,500, whereas for a couple it was $1,003,500. Many pensioner couples make the mistake of leaving all their assets to each other, which can cause a lot of grief when the surviving partner finds they have lost their pension as well as their partner.

CASE STUDY

Bob and Betty own their own home and have $780,000 in financial assets, as well as $20,000 in furniture and motor vehicles. They are assets-tested with total assessable assets of $800,000. They receive a part pension of $303.95 a fortnight each, which provides a total family pension income of $15,805 a year. They also receive all the concessions available to pensioners and part pensioners. Imagine the situation if Bob died suddenly and all their assets had been left to each other. On his death Betty would have total assets of $800,000, which would be way beyond the cut-off point for a single. In one fell swoop, she would have lost her pension, her husband, and all the concessions.

This is not a rare case. In fact, this situation is now so common that I am receiving many emails asking if it is possible to refuse a bequest, so as to preserve the status quo.

Unfortunately, it's not that simple. Centrelink staff tell me that a bequest from a deceased estate is not assessable by Centrelink until it is received, or able to be received, by the beneficiary. They accept that it may take up to 12 months for an estate to be finalised. The survivor needs to advise Centrelink of the date they receive, or become presently entitled to their bequest. See page 197 for an explanation of present entitlement.

If the estate has not been finalised after 12 months, Centrelink will consider what has caused the delay. If it can be proved that the delay was outside the beneficiary's control, it would still not be assessed at that time. However, if Centrelink believe that the beneficiary has contributed to the delay, the bequest would be regarded as available and therefore assessable.

It is certainly open to any beneficiary to decide that they do not wish to accept a bequest and make appropriate arrangements with the executor of the estate. However, Centrelink would treat the money forgone as a deprived asset: they would be subject to the deprivation rules for five years.

Therefore, if it is likely that you will receive an age pension at some stage, ensure that your will is set up to distribute assets in a way that optimises both tax and Centrelink outcomes. The easy way to do this is to leave part of your assets to your children, or other deserving beneficiaries. The survivor will have the satisfaction of sharing the joy with the other beneficiaries, instead of having to accept all the proceeds and the grief that may go with that. But think through your assets and how they are owned carefully; it's common for retirees to hold investments like shares as joint tenants. In circumstances like that, the shares owned by the deceased are transferred automatically to the survivor, irrespective of what is in the will.

It is complex — that's why a conversation with a good lawyer and financial planner is essential.

Trust assets

Occasionally I am asked if holding assets in a trust makes them exempt from Centrelink assessment. For most people the answer is no. When a trust structure is used, Centrelink apply both a control test and a source test. In the case of a trust, the control test is satisfied if an individual or an associate of that individual is a trustee of the trust, has the ability to remove other trustees, can vary the trust deed and can veto any decisions of the trustee. In other words, if a person has control over the trust Centrelink will regard the trust assets as their own, and the trust assets will be assessable.

The source test is concerned with the origin of the trust assets. It is satisfied when an individual has transferred property or services to the trust after the cut-off date, 7:30 PM on 9 May 2000, and the underlying transfer was made for less than the full value of the trust assets.

Aged care funding choices

The nature of aged care is such that many people are admitted to residential care prior to death, and die in aged care. The associated financing is a complex area, and advice from an aged care specialist is highly recommended.

RAD or DAP?

Typically, people in aged care have paid a refundable accommodation deposit (RAD), which is a lump-sum payment for a room (or part of a room) in an aged care home. On the death of the resident, the RAD will be refunded to the resident's estate.

If anyone has loaned money to pay the RAD, it is crucial to document it. There are lots of cases of beneficiaries claiming that the RAD was a loan to be repaid, and not general funds to be distributed in accordance with the will. Make sure any documentation is reviewed as soon as possible and vetted by your financial adviser or solicitor.

If someone is not expected to live very long in aged care, it may be best not to pay the RAD. The aged care facility can't refund it until the estate can provide a letter of administration or probate. However, the return of funds is government-guaranteed and the facility will pay interest on the RAD they are holding, first at 2.25% a year from the day after the resident leaves until the legislated time frame ends (generally 14 days from when they receive probate), then at the Maximum Permissible Interest Rate (MPIR), currently 8.38% a year.

The alternative is to pay a Daily Accommodation Payment (DAP), which is a method of paying interest on the RAD instead of making one upfront payment. The DAP amount is calculated by applying the MPIR to the room price and dividing the amount by 365 to reach the daily payment amount.

Sell or keep the family home?

A decision whether to sell or keep the family home is also of great importance. A common mistake made by the family or their attorney is to sell the family home to pay the RAD.

From an estate planning perspective, the big issue is that the home may be a specified asset; by selling it, you may cost the person it was left to their inheritance. I saw an example of an attorney wanting to sell Mum's house to pay her RAD. On reading the will it was noted that the house was a specified asset left to her daughter, with the son receiving all cash and investments. If the house had been sold to pay Mum's RAD it would have come back to the estate as cash, and on her death the son would have inherited everything, the daughter nothing. Undoubtedly a huge legal battle would have commenced. Once the attorney realised, they paid Mum's DAP.

From a spouse's perspective, the big issue is potential future cash flow issues. If one member of a couple is living in aged care and the other passes away leaving all assets and income to the person in aged care, the survivor will most likely see their means tested care fee go up, but they don't receive more care or any other benefit for the extra they pay. Obviously if they receive a pension that would also be impacted.

Even though the DAP (calculated at 8.38% on the unpaid RAD) can seem expensive, it can pale in comparison to these other costs. Firstly, if you keep the home it has a two-year assets test exemption for the age pension. If a spouse is still living there it is exempt for as long as they remain there, and for a further two years from the date they leave. The house is also only included in the aged care means test up to a capped value of $197,735 (whereas if it is sold, the full amount will usually be included, regardless of where you put it).

Means assessment

The means assessment is used to determine your loved one's liability to pay towards their accommodation and care costs. Often people enter aged care without completing a means assessment — if they die soon afterwards, the family may not know that it hasn't been done or may not realise that they need to do it.

Unless someone completes a means assessment for the person entering aged care (even if it is done post-death), they will be assessed as "means not disclosed" and be charged the full market price for their accommodation and the maximum means tested care fee (currently $400 a day, capped at $32,719 for the year). There have been cases of estates receiving huge bills for money they shouldn't have owed, because their loved one never completed the means test.

Investment bonds in estate planning

A major worry for many people planning their estate is the possibility of their estate being disputed. It's a valid concern because most assets — including superannuation — can be disputed. One effective strategy is to own an asset as joint tenants, in which case the remaining share of the asset passes to the co-owner on the death of the other owner. But in many situations, this would not be appropriate.

There is another strategy that cannot be disputed: put money into investment bonds. Their alternative name is insurance bonds, as many people confuse investment bonds with government bonds. Despite the confusing terminology, investment bonds have become the usual phrase for these products. They are a unique tool for leaving legacies, and not nearly as well-known as they should be.

Investment bonds are tax-paid investments like superannuation, but they don't have the drawbacks of superannuation. The government of the day always seems to be tampering with the superannuation rules and there is the possibility of a death tax if you die leaving money to non-dependants. Furthermore, if a bequest via superannuation is disputed, the estate may be tied up for years, not to mention the likely costs for any legal proceedings.

Both superannuation and investment bond funds pay tax on behalf of the investor, which means there is no need to include any income in the investor's yearly tax return.

However, there are certain critical differences. Superannuation funds pay tax on your behalf at 15%, investment bond funds pay 30%. The amount you can place in superannuation is limited, and your money is tied up until you satisfy a condition of release, such as reaching your preservation age (60 or more). There is no loss of access when you place your money in investment bonds, and the amount you can place in them is limitless.

Money invested in investment bonds comes from after-tax dollars. Because the earnings accrue within the fund there is no assessable income to declare on your tax return each year, and if you hold them for 10 years or more all proceeds can be redeemed tax-free.

If the investment bond is redeemed early, the proceeds are taxable as normal income but the holder is entitled to a tax offset of 30% to apply against other tax liabilities, which effectively makes investment bonds almost tax-free from personal tax for most investors. Suppose an investor earns $65,000 a year and cashes in an investment bond for $50,000, which cost them $40,000. With the $10,000 profit, the extra personal tax will be $3,250, but the offset will be $3,000 so the investor will have just $250 personal tax to pay.

They may offer capital gains tax advantages in some situations, as no personal CGT event is triggered on withdrawal.

CASE STUDY

Peter and Joan are a high-income couple — they invest $200,000 in an investment bond in Peter's name. Earnings will be taxed at just 30%. Because they believe the share market is at a low point, they ask for the entire investment to be placed in the Australian shares option. Three years later the market has surged, and they decide to take some profits. All they have to do is make a free switch from the share-based option to the more conservative cash option. No personal CGT is payable. Four years later Joan stops work to have a baby, and they decide to redeem the bond to renovate their home. Before cashing in the bond, Peter transfers it to Joan free of CGT, who cashes in the entire proceeds tax-free, as she earns no other income that year.

Nominating beneficiaries

As they are a form of life insurance policy, but linked to investment returns, an investment bond must have a life insured, which for estate purposes would typically be you. On your passing, the investment bond benefits would be paid to your estate or to your nominated beneficiary or beneficiaries.

An investment bond nominated in favour of a beneficiary is a non-estate asset and is therefore not subject to any directions under your will, disputes of your will, or any delays in the distribution and finalisation of your estate. The payment can be made confidentially, without the knowledge of other interested parties.

You may also be able to direct the investment bond provider to pass on the benefit payment to the estate of a nominated beneficiary instead. These features provide a convenient way to ensure that your nomination remains valid, irrespective of changes to the circumstances of your nominated beneficiaries. Some investment bonds provide the option of transferring ownership to another person, and in some cases you may be able to elect when the beneficiary gets access to the investment, as well as provide for a regular income stream to be paid in the future. The transfer of ownership can happen without any personal tax consequences for your investment or for the recipient of the investment bond.

Investment bonds are especially useful if you want to pass on wealth outside of your will and estate, pass on your wealth without incurring tax, want to manage when your intended recipient can access the investment and/or set up a future regular income stream for their use. The following case studies have been provided by Generation Life, one of Australia's leading providers of investment bonds.

CASE STUDY

Rachel is 60 and wants to provide for her family after her passing. She has two children, Sam and Louise, who have one and three children respectively. She wants to make sure enough funds are distributed to each of her children to help with the cost of raising the grandchildren. She is also trying to avoid conflict. She wants to provide $100,000 to Sam's family and $300,000 to Louise's family, to be paid after her death. She sets up an investment bond with an investment of $400,000 and is the sole life insured. She nominates that on her death Sam will receive 25% of the investment value and Louise will receive 75%.

The investment bond strategy allows her to bypass the estate and probate process to ensure that her wishes are met easily and promptly. If at any point in the future she wants to change how her investment is divided up, she can do so effortlessly without having to incur the cost of changing her will. Furthermore, if at some stage Rachel's circumstances change, such as a divorce or remarriage, there is no need for her to re-state or update the beneficiary details — the nominations will continue until she decides to change the nominated beneficiaries.

Don't forget that Louise's $400,000 initial investment, if she lives for 20 more years, may well be worth more than $1.3 million, which means her legacy will at least keep pace with the cost of living. Of course, if in 15 years' time the grandchildren need some money, possibly for a house deposit or university fees, she can cash in the investment bond in whole or part and take out whatever money she decides.

CASE STUDY

Barry, aged 80, is a wealthy retiree now happily remarried after a nasty divorce, who wants to leave a range of bequests to children of both marriages. He is aware that there is acrimony between some family members, and it is extremely important to him that his assets on death be split and distributed in the way he wishes and not eroded by family legal battles.

He invests $250,000 in his own name in each of five separate investment bonds, naming each of the five children as the beneficiary of one investment bond upon his death. Because an investment bond is technically a life policy, the proceeds must be paid directly to the beneficiary outside of the estate finalisation process and Barry can sleep soundly in the knowledge he has solved the potential litigation problem in advance.

Alternative to a testamentary trust

Investment bonds can be a great alternative to a testamentary trust, with the flexibility to meet future funding needs of your loved ones without the complexity often arising from testamentary trusts. The investment bond has several unique features, which include:

- not requiring to be set up under a will
- no additional establishment costs, unlike a testamentary trust
- not requiring the appointment of a willing and competent trustee
- can be structured to make small and large value gifts with no ongoing tax reporting or other administrative tasks.

Some investment bond providers can establish a future ownership arrangement for your children, grandchildren or any person that you want to look after. The investment bond can be structured to provide access to funds in the future after your passing, with the added ability for you to determine when access to funds will be available. With some providers, you can also choose whether you want to provide full access to funds or provide a regular payment or income stream.

This feature can come in handy, particularly if you have loved ones that may require a disciplined approach to managing their financial affairs after you're gone.

Even with the best of planning, as with many things in life, there will inevitably be unexpected events or circumstances that require access to funds. Again, there are providers that will enable you to restrict future access to funds but still provide flexibility for your loved one to make withdrawals, provided you've appointed a trusted person to authorise these special one-off withdrawal requests.

CASE STUDY

Margo is 86 and has a devoted grandson, Jack, aged 24, who is not so good at managing his finances. Margo wants to help her grandson financially for his future but is concerned that Jack may waste a lump sum of money. Margo also wants to delay his inheritance until he is older, but make sure that if he needs access to funds for special needs (such as a first home deposit) Jack can get access.

Margo sets up an investment bond to the value of $100,000 to help Jack, with a future transfer arrangement so that her investment bond's ownership passes to Jack when he turns 40. She instructs that Jack should receive a regular annual payment equal to 10% of the value of the investment at the time of transfer, until the funds are depleted. Margo also nominates her friends from bridge club, Henry and Jan, whom she trusts, to authorise any special one-off payments that Jack requests in the future.

Margo's investment bond meets her goals in helping her grandson, while retaining control even after her passing without the need for complex trust structures and additional costs. Margo is also free to change her arrangements before her passing if things change for Jack.

Grandchildren's education

A major part of estate planning is leaving a legacy. Many people want to leave money for their grandkids' education. But there are obstacles to this everywhere you turn.

For starters, most institutions will not accept investments in the name of a minor, and if the money is held by a parent or grandparent as trustee for a child, the trustee can be liable for children's tax, which is set at punitive rates — as high as 66% once income from the investment exceeds a paltry $416 a year. If you try to get around children's tax by investing in the name of either parent, the income from the investment can adversely affect family tax payments, push them into a higher tax bracket or hinder eligibility for superannuation co-contributions. If a grandparent invests in their own name, they could lose some aged pension as the investment grows in value.

Investment bonds are the perfect solution. All you have to do is make an investment into the investment bond and sit back and watch it grow. Then, once you have owned the investment bond for 10 years, you can withdraw all or part of the proceeds free of personal tax. However, there is no obligation to withdraw your money and you can leave it in the low tax investment bond area for as long as you wish.

When taking out this type of investment, it is customary to nominate an age or date when the investment will automatically vest in the name of the child. This can be at any stage or date, provided the child is between 10 years and 25 years. If there is no nomination, it automatically passes to the child at age 25.

CASE STUDY

The grandparents want to start an investment plan for their grandchild and are prepared to start it off with an initial investment of $10,000. They hope to be able to make additional investments, but do not want to be put in a position where they could be forced to do so. After talking to their financial adviser they decide to use an investment bond in the name of the mother, with the child as the life insured, and a nominated vesting age of 21.

Now comes the best part. By holding the investment bond in this way, the parent has absolute discretion as to when funds will be placed in the child's name. Until the investment bond is actually transferred to the child, the parent as policy holder has full control over the investment, including changing the vesting age. Furthermore, there is no capital gains tax on the transfer.

Can you think of a more perfect intergenerational investment? The mother has total control, there is no annual income generated, and the money is available at call even if the child has not reached vesting age.

I cannot stress highly enough that this is a complex area, and this chapter provides nothing more than a brief overview. You should always seek expert advice, because getting it wrong can be costly. A good financial adviser will think about the taxes you pay today, into the future and upon your eventual demise. Intergenerational wealth and tax planning done well can have immense value, so be sure to encourage your advisers in the legal, financial, and taxation fields to collaborate effectively and openly.

Equity release

Rising life expectancies and mounting inflation mean that many retirees may be pressed for cash after they retire. All political parties are aware of this, and there is a consensus that retirees should rely on the equity in their home, as well as other assets, to see them through retirement. There are two ways to do this.

1. **Downsize to a cheaper home.** This strategy often has the major disadvantage of converting part of an exempt asset — the family home — to an assessable asset. If you are receiving a part age pension now, increasing your assessable assets could mean a substantial reduction in your pension, or even the loss of it. To make matters worse, the costs of moving from one home to another are high, which usually means a net loss of capital. Most importantly, many retirees want to remain in their local communities and it may be hard to find a good-quality smaller home nearby. These issues are discussed in detail in my book *Retirement Made Simple*.

2. **Remain in the home and free up capital** by either taking out a reverse mortgage or using one of the other products that transfer part of the equity in your home in exchange for cash. In this book, I will just explain reverse mortgages, as they are the most common form of equity release in Australia. The other methods can be quite complex, and you should take expert advice if you think that may be the best way to go.

A conventional mortgage is not a practical option for most retirees. Being asset rich and cash poor, they cannot afford the recurring loan repayments, and most would have trouble getting a loan because of their age and lack of paid work. This is where the "reverse mortgage" comes in. It's designed for retirees because there are no regular repayments of principal or interest unless you wish to make them. As a result, the loan will compound, increasing faster and faster as time passes.

The big benefit of a reverse mortgage is flexibility. Monies could be drawn down as a lump sum, or in monthly payments, as a type of income. A line of credit is available within the approved facility to cater for any future expenses. No interest applies to the line of credit until funds are drawn. Reverse mortgages in Australia have a "no negative equity" guarantee, which means that if the sale proceeds of the property are less than the loan outstanding, a lender cannot make claims on any shortfall. Despite these consumer protections, it is prudent to check if there are any exclusions from the guarantee, or any circumstances in which it can be lost.

Additional consumer protections include the requirement for all borrowers to seek independent legal advice on their mortgage documents. The solicitor will go to great lengths to ensure that you understand this complex financial decision — and if they don't, see one that does! This is a significant financial decision, which should be taken with great care and with the assistance of trusted advisers. It is also important to prepare or review wills and enduring powers of attorney.

CASE STUDY

A couple aged 75 with a home worth $1 million take out a reverse mortgage of $100,000 at 8.5%. The home increases at 3% a year and no repayments are made on the reverse mortgage, so in 15 years the house is worth $1.55 million, with a loan against it of around $350,000, resulting in a net equity of around $1.2 million.

By this stage, the couple are 90 years of age, and they decide the house is too big for them. It is time to downsize. They can pay off the debt from the sale proceeds. Alternatively, they may let the debt keep increasing, secure in the knowledge there is still plenty of equity, which the beneficiaries will receive tax-free.

Common uses of reverse mortgages include a monthly drawdown to top up retirement income or setting aside a contingency fund for future needs. More and more retirees are now retiring with an outstanding balance on their home loan or credit card, and a reverse mortgage can refinance this debt without depleting retirement income. Another major use of home equity is to renovate the family home to enjoy another 20 years of lifestyle at home and improve the value of a CGT-exempt asset at the same time. Think about it: if you love living where you are, even if you need $75,000 for home maintenance, a reverse mortgage may be a better option than going to all the expense and inconvenience of changing properties.

If you have your own funding and housing well sorted for the long term, you can also give lump sums withdrawn from home equity to kids for their own first home deposit (a great investment) or for your grandchildren's education (which yields lifetime earnings). Already the "Bank of Mum and Dad" is Australia's fifth-biggest bank, but often at the expense of mum and dad's retirement nest egg. Responsible intergenerational transfers of home equity can give help when kids need it most. Now that retirees live, on average, to almost 90, most children can't expect a bequest before their mid-60s — too late to make a big difference to their lives. And finally, reverse mortgages are playing a big role in funding healthcare costs — both for in-home care and for residential aged care — which are woefully underfunded by the government.

Be judicious about your gifting decisions if you are a full or part pensioner, however. Any amount over $10,000 gifted in one year, with a maximum of $30,000 over five years, will be treated as a deprived asset by Centrelink for five years. There are thresholds for both assets and income, and specialist reverse mortgage advisers will be able to discuss scenarios.

Remember that when you take out a reverse mortgage, you are accessing money today that will result in leaving less to your estate when you die. It's not just the money you actually use, it's the compounding effect that means the interest on the debt will grow as time passes. A great way to stop that happening is for family who can afford it to pay the interest. This would be in the family's interest because the loan on the house would not increase. But of course, every possible strategy has challenges: maybe some of the family would have the resources to pay the interest but others have not. If the family get on well, they could draw up an agreement that the sale proceeds of the house will first be used to reimburse the interest to the children who paid it.

Understand that a reverse mortgage could have a major effect on the amount of money that you leave behind you, which is why it's important to involve your beneficiaries. People have such different viewpoints on this: some may say, "You enjoy it. You've earned it; we don't need the money", while others may see the value of the family home as their right and fight anything that would reduce it every step of the way. Communication is essential.

Checklist for equity release

- ☐ Are you making this decision freely and voluntarily? Does anyone (including a family member) have a strong influence on your decision?
- ☐ Have you reviewed the transaction with your solicitor, accountant, financial adviser, and family?
- ☐ Have you investigated the product beyond the marketing material, i.e. done your due diligence, including checking that the fund's provider has an Australian Financial Services Licence?
- ☐ What is the impact of the transaction on your pension or other government benefits?
- ☐ Will accessing equity in your home now reduce your ability to pay for services in the future, such as aged care, medical expenses and general living expenses?
- ☐ Does the agreement impact on your freedom to sell or move out of your home, e.g. does leaving the home start payment obligations to the lender?
- ☐ If you move out, does the agreement allow for other family members to remain in the home?
- ☐ Does this agreement affect your power of attorney?
- ☐ What impact does this agreement have on your will? Is there an estate left to bequeath?

Implications for your will

Equity release has major implications for your estate planning, so if you choose to release the equity in your home by way of a reverse mortgage you should review your will and power of attorney at the same time.

Have you left your property as a specific gift to one person upon your death? If so, the will must be reviewed in the light of which beneficiaries have their inheritance affected by the equity release repayment.

When you pass away, it is likely that your executor will sell your home. If you have a reverse mortgage, a chunk of the sale proceeds will go towards repaying the mortgage, plus any fees or charges from the lender. This may deplete your estate significantly, leaving your beneficiaries with very little inheritance.

Are you using the money from the reverse mortgage to assist one child? If so, do you need to equalise the effect on that of your other children in your will? If you choose to do nothing, you risk the other children contesting the will.

It is possible to restrict the types and scope of financial decisions your attorney can make on your behalf. If you take on a reverse mortgage, it is essential that you review the powers you have given them, as it may be necessary to remove some restrictions to enable them to deal with the lender on your behalf.

If you lose capacity and must move into care, your attorney is the person who can sell the house for you and has to deal with the lender. If nobody has that authority when you lose capacity, an application will have to be made to the respective Guardianship Tribunal in your state or territory for a guardian and administrator to be appointed.

Finally, with aged care, a reverse mortgage specific for the purpose of aged care is available for a five-year term. It is important to understand that the former home is an exempt asset only for the first two years, unless a protected person still resides there. Once again, you should seek specific professional advice.

Multigenerational living (granny flats)

Senior Australians often choose to age with family, rather than in an aged care facility. They may be prompted by loneliness, especially loss of a spouse, increasing costs of living, or difficulty coping with day-to-day needs, and "granny flat" is a term you will hear more often as the population ages. It is such a simple term that you may not give it a second thought. But if you think that a granny flat is a self-contained dwelling you make in your home for your older relations, so all you have to worry about is building regulations, that is a dangerous misapprehension.

There are many success stories for these arrangements, but these are not the ones that make the news (or the courts). It is important to go into these transactions understanding their risks, as when they go wrong the older person may be left penniless, even homeless, and adult children may find themselves in financial trouble because they are trying to do the right thing caring for a parent.

Unfortunately, multigenerational living in a granny flat has become one of the most complex areas of financial and estate planning. A good starting point to understand its ins and outs is the book *Downsizing Made Simple*, by Rachel Lane and myself, but having read that you will still need to get good advice. Granny flats are an area where failing to plan is tantamount to planning to fail. My main goal in this section is to alert you to some of the complex issues involved.

For starters, you need to understand that the terminology is confusing:

- "granny flat" doesn't describe a type of property
- "a granny flat right or interest" doesn't actually exist as a legal right.

You can have a granny flat interest in any kind of property: it doesn't just apply to the properties often referred to as "granny flats", and it is not necessarily a separate room or area in the family home. What you cannot have, is a granny flat interest in a property you legally own. This includes property that you, your partner, or a trust or company you control owns.

You create a granny flat interest when you exchange assets, money, or both, for a right to live in someone's property for life. This right only lasts for your lifetime: it is not part of your estate when you die. A "granny flat agreement", sanctioned by the national insurer Lexon, is an increasingly popular option, so seek a lawyer who is familiar with how to prepare them. If you convey an interest in your current home to an adult child as either a joint tenant or tenant in common, it is not a "granny flat interest" but could be set up as an "assets for care" arrangement.

The other options are a life tenancy or a right to reside, which are explained in detail on pages 108–111, and can create quite different outcomes if at any stage you want to move out of the granny flat.

There are three common ways to establish a granny flat right/interest.

1. **The parents remain living in their own home** and transfer ownership to an adult child, who moves into the property. The adult child, with their family, if they have one, agrees to provide companionship and care in exchange for the asset. Remember, if the parents retain ownership or part-ownership of the property, a granny flat right has not been established.

2. **The parents sell their home** and pay for a self-contained unit to be built at the adult child's property, or for modifications to the existing home.

3. **Both parents and children sell their existing homes** and buy a new home in the children's names. If the new home is bought in the parents' names, a granny flat right has not been established.

There are three main areas where problems may occur — family emotions, Centrelink issues and, in some cases, capital gains tax.

Family emotions and granny flats

Families often establish a granny flat after the death of one parent, for the widow or widower, or when there are clear signs of deteriorating health in one or both parents. But be extremely wary of leaping into a granny flat arrangement — it is often perceived as an easy option, but it can tear a family apart.

Typically, a granny flat right is made within a family: the younger generation provide accommodation and care in exchange for a payment or transfer of assets. And when they work well, they often work very well. Far too often, however, problems arise. The most common ones we hear about are:

- the carer child's situation becomes difficult because
  - they divorce, start a new relationship, become ill, or want to travel
  - the parent becomes too frail, or their dementia too advanced, for home care
- the other children's situation becomes difficult because
  - they feel that their inheritance has been stolen
  - they don't believe the quality of care provided by their sibling is up to standard

- their relationship with their sibling becomes difficult and as a result they become estranged from their parent.

These emotional complications can blow up into major feuds amazingly quickly. The best way to minimise this risk is to get the whole family talking before going into a granny flat arrangement.

Centrelink issues with granny flats

Social security provisions allow people to transfer assets well over the normal gifting limits in exchange for a right to life occupancy in a residential property. However, there are limits around the amount that may be paid, and once the limits are exceeded the amount above the limit will be treated as a gift to the children.

For Centrelink purposes it must be:

- all or part of a private residence
- your principal home
- not owned by you, your partner or a trust or company you control.

The amount paid for a granny flat determines homeowner or non-homeowner status for Centrelink's pension assets test and whether or not the older person can qualify for rent assistance.

If the home is transferred for the granny flat, pension entitlement would remain unchanged, as the asset position remains the same. If the proceeds from the sale of the home and assets outside the home are used to purchase the granny flat, pension entitlement would likely increase.

When the parents sell their home, which is an exempt asset for Centrelink, the proceeds are converted to cash, which may be assessable for Centrelink. However, the amount they contribute to the home of their children may not be assessable for Centrelink, depending on the amount. But of course the parents' home is now lost to the estate, and the money spent on the granny flat in the children's house becomes part of the child's assets.

Therefore, a major part of the parents' assets may be lost to the estate. This may not be an issue if the child is an only child or if all the siblings agree that this is the best strategy long-term. But if some children think one of the siblings has received favourable treatment to the detriment of others, there could be major conflicts. Make sure you discuss your plans with all your children, and if necessary, compensate the child or children who did not benefit from the sale of your home with additional cash or asset bequests to "even up" the distribution. Then update your will as required. The alternative could be your remaining children making a family provision application for better provision from your estate.

Another trap is that if you establish a granny flat arrangement within five years of moving into aged care and it was "reasonably foreseeable" that the older person would need to move into care, any sum paid for the granny flat may be considered a gift and treated as a deprived asset.

The most important piece of advice is to secure your financial interest in the property and carefully document the agreement with the assistance of a solicitor.

Capital gains tax on granny flats

When parents remain living in their own home and transfer ownership to an adult child who moves into the property, if the child already owned a home of their own, they may rent it out for up to six years and it will retain its CGT exemption, or they may sell the house within six months, CGT exempt, and invest the money elsewhere.

However, it is important to realise that if the granny flat right is not created properly, it will trigger a CGT event for the property owner, with no cost base to subtract, and the sale proceeds being the rent over the parent's life expectancy. Further, if the granny flat is neither considered part of the family home nor owned by the occupier, then when it is eventually sold on the open market, it will not be covered by anyone's main residence CGT exemption.

Other options for multigenerational living

Julia Hartman points out that in many situations a simpler solution is for the parents and children to each take an ownership interest in the property they will share. The parent's share will be covered by their main residence exemption and still exempt from consideration for Centrelink purposes. If things go wrong and the property has to be sold, the parent has some clearly quantifiable rights. The ownership interest can be joint tenancy so that it simply rolls over to the children when the parent dies, or tenants in common so that it can become part of the parent's estate to even things up with the other children.

Traditional property ownership laws are well tested, unlike granny flat arrangements, which may therefore be more open to legal challenges. Ownership rights are far more equitable, for example, giving the parent the right to force a sale if they are being mistreated. This arrangement is therefore more likely to lead to a harmonious relationship that is in everyone's interest.

Protecting your estate

What happens in the unfortunate event that your family member, or the owner of the house in which you have a financial interest, suddenly passes away? If the agreement does not "bind the estates" of all of the parties to the agreement, their executor is not obliged to repay your financial contribution.

In the absence of a properly documented agreement, another issue for older people who have embarked on an "assets for care" arrangement is the old legal concept of "presumption of advancement". This is the legal presumption that the transfer of an asset or a cash payment from a parent to a child is a gift, unless the parent can prove a contrary intention at the time of the transfer, e.g. "I contributed $250,000 to the cost of the home in return for a lifetime of care". The difficulty is, if the relationship has broken down several years into the arrangement and it comes time to prove the intention or the motivation behind the transfer, the older person's capacity is often impaired and they are unable to provide sufficient evidence. If the older person or their representatives are not in a position to pursue the issue through the court process, the money is often lost.

But in other situations, a granny flat right can be used to protect the estate.

CASE STUDY

Mary is a widow aged 75 — she receives the full age pension because her only assets are her home and $75,000 in a credit union. Her favourite daughter is Tess, who is single and who lives with her. Unfortunately, there is family conflict with some of the siblings. Mary is concerned her will may be disputed after she dies and Tess could end up with nowhere to live.

Mary transfers the house to Tess as a gift in exchange for Tess giving Mary the right to live in that house until Mary dies. A granny flat right has been effected and Mary has the right to live there as long as she's able. She can rest secure in the knowledge that the house should be safe from any challenges to the estate.

Just be aware that New South Wales has more onerous laws than the other states. If the transaction above took place less than three years before Mary's death, there is potential for a claim on the estate under the notional estate principle. This means that any assets disposed of within three years could be brought back into the estate assets for distribution purposes. This is another reason to get your estate planning done sooner rather than later.

Risk of elder abuse

Financial and psychological abuse are the top two types of abuse that is perpetrated on older people. Victims are generally widowed women in their 80s, and the perpetrators of the abuse are equally split between adult sons and adult daughters aged in their 50s.

As discussed earlier, misuse of powers of attorney is a key method of abuse. Another prevalent form of financial abuse is an adult child convincing an elderly or impaired parent to transfer or sell their home. These sorts of situations often occur after the adult child has successfully isolated their parent from other family members.

Housing affordability and the general lack of housing has led to a rise in "inheritance impatience". This is essentially adult children who can't afford their own home or who are struggling with their mortgage repayments eyeing off their parents' mortgage-free home as an easy way out of their mortgage stress. Why wait until their parents pass away? Quite often such a granny flat agreement is not in the older person's interest and overwhelmingly benefits the adult child.

Obtaining some objective and independent advice from a solicitor and your accountant is the best way to reality check an adult child's great idea to relieve you of your home in the form of an early inheritance.

Checklist for multigenerational living

- ☐ Are you making this decision freely and voluntarily? Are you being influenced by a family member who is in immediate financial difficulty?
- ☐ Who owns the house you are moving into or paying the mortgage of?
- ☐ Does the agreement include the names of all of the property owners?
- ☐ Is your financial contribution recognised by being named on title, or by a registered mortgage on the property?
- ☐ Have you obtained advice on the transaction from your solicitor, accountant, financial adviser, and all family members?
- ☐ Are you clear on the taxation implications of the agreement?

- ☐ How will it affect your Centrelink or Department of Veterans' Affairs pension?
- ☐ Can the agreement be terminated? In what circumstances?
- ☐ Can you get your money back to pay an accommodation deposit at an aged care facility?
- ☐ What happens if the property is sold, e.g. family breakdown and a property settlement?
- ☐ Do you have access to the entire house? Do you have privacy?
- ☐ Who will cover which household expenses? Detail this carefully.
- ☐ Does the agreement allow you to live in the property for life?
- ☐ Are there any circumstances that would lead to you being evicted from the property?
- ☐ What happens if your care needs increase? Can you obtain in-home care or do you have to move into aged care?
- ☐ Have you documented the agreement, engaging a lawyer experienced in these aspects of elder law?
- ☐ Does the agreement bind the estates of all the parties?
- ☐ What impact does this agreement have on your will?

Digital assets and death

So many things are now done online that taking care of your digital life is an important new requirement for executors and attorneys. Some accounts — like online banking — are just means of accessing your assets, others actually hold content that you have created, curated, and/or shared — like your photographs. They may also be an important way in which you keep in touch with friends, which should be accessed and updated when you pass, and that hold content you would like to remain accessible only to those you shared it with.

When considering digital assets, it is important to first determine if the asset can be distributed under a will, i.e. is it transferable (which is rare), or is it merely a personal right or licence that ends on death? Most digital accounts are not "property" and are therefore not owned by you but by the business operating the online platform.

On the other hand, if you are storing your own creations online — and "creations" includes business papers, personal documents, photos, etc. — you probably hold the copyright in these works. Copyright could be an asset of some value to your heirs, or simply content that the family would prefer to retain privately.

What is a digital asset?

- social media accounts, e.g. Facebook, Instagram, LinkedIn or X (formerly Twitter)
- email accounts
- streaming services, e.g. Spotify, Netflix, Audible
- cloud data storage, e.g. iCloud or OneDrive
- loyalty programs, e.g. airline frequent flyer or store reward schemes
- online payment accounts, e.g. PayPal.

Unfortunately there is no one law covering what happens to digital assets on death. Therefore it is necessary to consider each provider's individual terms and conditions, or terms of use.

Facebook and Instagram provide an ability for users to appoint a "legacy contact", through their accounts centre. This enables a family member to access your account in order to transfer its contents and delete it.

Google permits users to set up an "inactive account manager". This enables a person to deal with email accounts or any other accounts held with Google for the purposes of closing these accounts.

Most airline and store loyalty programs are not transferable on death, and the points will revert to the provider unless you have made other arrangements beforehand, e.g. transferring your points to a family member prior to your passing (if permitted by the terms of use).

During your estate planning, it is very helpful to list your digital assets and make appropriate arrangements to ensure that your executor — or another friend or family member — can access these accounts so they may be closed or deleted. Furthermore, consider consolidating your passwords into a password manager, which is relatively easy to keep updated and provide to your executor for access.

Funeral arrangements

Death comes to all of us, but most people prefer to leave thinking about it until another day. As a result, most of us are unprepared for the important decisions that have to be made when someone dies, and may suffer a lot of unnecessary stress.

Immediately after someone you love dies, you will find yourself thrown into a whirlwind of activity. For some people this is another blow, for others it serves as a beneficial distraction.

> *A great deal of money is expended on funerals and that, in itself, seems to betray a lack of confidence in the resurrection of the dead.*
>
> *Rev. Edward Henderson*

When a death occurs

Most deaths occur at a hospital, aged care home, or residence of the deceased. The first step is to ensure that a doctor certifies the death. If death happens at home, you probably have a palliative care doctor's details on hand, and you should call them straight away.

The next step is to get in touch with a funeral director. They will arrange to transfer the body, and can begin making the necessary arrangements, including registering the death and applying for a death certificate. Many people die in the early hours, but you are not obliged to call the funeral director until business hours.

The death needs to be registered with the Births Deaths and Marriages Registry in the state or territory where the person died. Once registered, a death certificate is issued, generally in around three to four weeks.

Planning a funeral

Some people plan their funerals well in advance, but most don't. This is an emotional time, so consider asking another family member or friend to help you with this administrative process.

The first meeting with the funeral director can take place at their office or in your home. In order to carry out their role, the funeral director will need basic information about the deceased, such as their full name, address, occupation, place and date of death. It would be helpful to take along the deceased's birth certificate or passport, and marriage certificate.

The funeral director is also usually responsible for arranging appropriate newspaper notices and booking a suitable venue, church, cemetery, or crematorium for the funeral. They may also advise and assist you with such details as religious and ceremonial requirements and other funeral customs.

Having a clear understanding of the deceased's wishes as they relate to their funeral is invaluable, particularly at this emotional time.

Funeral decisions

Depending on the deceased's wishes, a funeral can be informal or formal and can take place in a range of venues, including a church, the chapel of the funeral home, the crematorium, or at the grave.

A READER'S TALE

When my dad was dying, we had no idea if he wanted to be buried or cremated and where. I asked him on his death bed — which was tough. He chose to be cremated, but because there was no one else there at the time, my family was somewhat doubtful about what his wishes were. We learnt our lesson, and made sure that there were family discussions with Mum well before she passed away.

When she did pass, her funeral was all organised and we had even bought the plot.

Upon meeting with the funeral director, there are a number of decisions to be made, including:

- Burial or cremation?
- Time and place of the funeral and cremation/burial. Note that these are usually held at the same time, but they can be separated if that suits your circumstances better.
- Casket (rectangular, and dearer than a coffin), coffin (tapered at each end) or something else — some places now offer winding sheets, wicker caskets and various other options.
- Do you want a viewing of the deceased, also called an "open casket"? About 15% of families choose to do this. What clothing will the deceased be buried in? Obviously, viewing the body is a choice for each family but there is some evidence of positive reactions being felt by those who had been through the viewing experience. Funeral directors recommend you have the viewing if you are in any doubt. Then you will not have regrets later, when it is too late to do it.
- Funeral service — religious or non-religious? Who will give the eulogy? Who else will speak? Floral arrangements? Music? Does the event need to be streamed online for mourners at a distance?
- Transport of the coffin/casket to the venue.

The cost of the funeral

The cost of a funeral can vary considerably, therefore it is essential to obtain a written estimate so that you can compare prices with other providers. On most occasions a deposit will be required.

Do review the quote carefully with the funeral director to make sure that you understand what the cost includes and what it does not. Generally speaking, the funeral costs include the coffin or casket, all disbursements such as advertising, church fees, and burial certificates, as well as the funeral director's charges for doing all the work from transporting and preparing the body to arranging the funeral. Additional costs may include burial plots, cremation niches and headstones.

There are also a number of pre-planned payment options for funerals, which I discuss below.

Most banks will reimburse the executor, from the deceased's account, for the cost of the funeral on presentation of the death certificate and the invoice or receipt for payment. However, as with all interactions with banks and other financial institutions, it is prudent to check this before committing to spending your own money on a funeral.

Again, it is worthwhile to take along a friend or family member to assist you during this process as there are a lot of detailed decisions that need to be made.

READER TIP: ASK SOMEONE LESS CLOSE TO ARRANGE THE FUNERAL

Arranging a funeral after the death of a close family member such as a husband, wife, mother, father or child is incredibly traumatic. On top of the grief, you are expected to be on top of all of the required paperwork and also make detailed arrangements for the funeral. You are often left with no time to grieve as you are consumed with the "death administration". Consider asking a sister- or brother-in-law, close friend, or relative who is not so directly impacted by the death to either assist or take over the funeral arrangements. My father died very suddenly and my sister-in-law stepped in and took over these arrangements. It was such a gift to us all to then be able to grieve rather than organise.

READER TIP: FIND ALL THE DATA

I organised my father's cremation. It was a simple process but required quite a lot of detailed personal information, which I would advise people to gather before someone is likely to pass away, including places and date of marriage, birth, mother's name, etc. Much of this was not well known as we had migrated to Australia many years ago.

Paying for the funeral

Some people prefer to make arrangements for their funeral when they are alive. And in some cases, you can get an increase in your age pension by putting money into some kind of funeral plan.

There are three basic options for financing the funeral.

1. **Pay after death.** After death occurs, meet with a funeral director and make all the arrangements for the funeral. At this time you're normally required to pay 50% of the price with the balance payable later.
2. **Pre-pay the funeral.** In this case, you have a similar meeting with the funeral director, make arrangements and pay for the funeral there and then. The price is then fixed, irrespective of how long it is before the death.

3. **Get a funeral bond.** Put a sum of money into a funeral bond, with the intention that money will be used to pay for the funeral when death eventually occurs.

Let's think about these now.

READER TIP: PLAN THE FUNERAL BEFORE YOU NEED TO

If possible, before the person dies, give the hospital written instructions for the direct dispatch of the body from the hospital to the funeral home of your choice. They will want the hospital bed back in use as soon as possible. You can also organise direct cremation, which means the crematorium collects the body, organises the necessary paperwork through their own funeral director, and delivers the ashes direct to your home so you can organise a memorial service, rather than using a public venue organised by a funeral home provider.

If the person dies with no instructions on where to send the body, some hospitals have an agreement with a local funeral home to pick up the body and place it in care for a hefty fee (like $1,500) until you make a decision which provider you are going to use. So, if you want best choice for the least costs make a decision beforehand and tell the hospital in writing!

I found a good website to review funeral home prices and services that was set up a few years ago by an accountant after he got the emotional run-around and pressure tactics when one of his parents died. It's called ***Gathered Here*** (***www.gatheredhere.com.au***). I read about the website in the *Australian Financial Review* — as my mother was dying. The story was about how the big commercial funeral homes tried to take the website to court to close it down over its publishing of "commercial in confidence" fees and services.

READER TIP: SHOP AROUND FOR FUNERALS

Funerals can be excessively expensive but there are low cost "no frills" services who will collect the deceased and arrange a modest funeral or cremation. These services generally don't advertise extensively (if at all) so you have to look for them. They generally are not in shiny city or suburban offices but a little out of the city. We found one on the Central Coast about an hour from Sydney where my mother passed away. My mother requested no funeral, but just to be cremated and her ashes scattered at her beloved beach. It wasn't about the money — she was just very no-fuss. My sister-in-law had done some ringing around for quotes and they ranged from $5000 to $10,000 even after explaining the desired simplicity. Some didn't even offer such a simple service. She then stumbled on a small company who collected our mother, cremated her and delivered the ashes for around $2,500. This level of simplicity does not suit everyone, but it was exactly what we wanted. The family had a memorial lunch and scattered her ashes at the beach just as she wished.

Paying after death

The benefit of this strategy is that it's simple. It also avoids the possibility of making arrangements in advance that are never enacted.

Sadly, it's not uncommon for people to buy a funeral bond, or prepay the funeral, but forget to tell anybody about what they have done. When death occurs, which could be years later, the executor can't find — or doesn't even know they should look for — the required paperwork.

Unless you are a meticulous record keeper, it is all too easy for key documents to get lost. A common occurrence is for someone to lose capacity and move from the family home to an aged care facility. Their home may be full of all sorts of accumulated paperwork, and important documents get lost in the muddle when the family is emptying the house to prepare it for sale.

It's also possible that the cost of a funeral may increase so much due to inflation that the financial outcome might have been better if they had pre-paid the funeral or invested in a funeral bond.

Pre-paid funeral

When you arrange a pre-paid funeral, you usually have a meeting with the funeral director to decide what you wish to spend on your funeral, and the type of funeral you want. You then join a funeral plan and nominate a specific funeral director on your plan certificate.

Parents of blended families often like to put a pre-paid funeral plan in place to minimise disagreements about what their loved one should have for the service. Bear in mind that once you pre-pay the funeral, the entire service is arranged. In this way it is quite different to a funeral bond.

However, the family is tied to the funeral company that has contracted to arrange the funeral.

Funeral bonds

Another popular way to provide for your funeral is to invest some money in a funeral bond, which allows you to set aside money to cover your funeral costs. This is an investment offered by specialist companies, such as Generation Life. A funeral bond provides benefits only upon the death of the nominated person and cannot be accessed prior to death.

This is a highly effective investment, particularly for pensioners, and helps to ensure you cover an essential element in your estate planning: paying for your funeral. A major benefit is that the fund in which the money is invested is a tax-exempt fund, which enables your savings in this area to grow in a tax-free environment. Leading funeral bond funds are conservatively run, and your money is secure.

For pension eligibility purposes, neither the growing value of the asset nor the bonuses that are added each year are taken into account. This enables pensioners to transfer assets to a tax-exempt area where it does not reduce their pension. Furthermore, they gain peace of mind knowing their funeral is taken care of.

You can buy funeral bonds through licensed security dealers. The funeral bond brochure will contain a form that enables you to transfer the ownership of the policy to a nominated funeral director, but this cannot take effect until after death.

The drawbacks? They are slight. You lose access to the money, which in many cases is a good thing anyway, and there is a limit of $15,000 on how much you can invest. There is also a requirement that the money be used for genuine funeral expenses. If not, these bonds would degenerate into another "tax fiddle".

CASE STUDY

Mr and Mrs Kelly decide that $7,500 each is a reasonable price for their funerals. They invest $7,500 each into a funeral bond. As they are assets-tested pensioners, those funds become exempt for the assets test — their pension will increase by $22.50 a week. That's not only covered the funeral costs, but they also receive an effective return of 7.8% a year on the $15,000 invested.

Overfunding

It is important to heed your adviser when investing in funeral bonds, because different fund managers have different requirements. A funeral bond can fund only one funeral, but they are often taken out in joint names. If the bond is in joint names and one party dies, the survivor has the option of keeping the bond intact for his or her own funeral, or cashing it in immediately to pay for the first funeral. If someone passes away overseas and does not use the funeral bond — or a pre-paid funeral — the estate will receive a full refund of the money paid, on production of the death certificate.

Some fund managers insist on a copy of the death certificate and an account from the funeral director so they know how much to pay out. Any excess funds are forfeited by the estate. Other managers are happy to pay excess funds to the estate. These funds interpret the tax laws differently and believe the limit of $15,000 imposed on any one investor is sufficient restriction to ensure the tax-free status of the bonds is not abused.

Avoid funeral insurance

With funeral cover, plans and insurance, you make regular ongoing payments until you pass away. When you've passed, your family receives some money to cover the cost of your funeral. The ASIC website, ***moneysmart.gov.au***, warns against these products. They point out that you may end up paying a lot more than the actual cover you will get. For example, if you start paying for funeral cover when you or your family are very young, you might end up paying a lot more than a funeral would cost. A savings account or a pre-paid funeral might cost you less for the same funeral. What's worse is that, if you miss payments or cancel the policy, you might not get a refund — you could lose all the money you paid.

Action list

- ☐ Review your estate planning with the greater knowledge you have gained from this chapter to see if you need to explore making any changes.
- ☐ If your family situation has changed since you last reviewed your affairs, make an appointment to do it now.
- ☐ Consider whether investment bonds might fit your situation.
- ☐ Include details about your digital assets in the information you provide to your executor and/or attorney, and appoint a digital legacy contact for your key digital accounts.
- ☐ Consider your funeral plans and discuss your wishes with your family.

7

Your end game

I hope that you will not be one of the large number of Australians who die without an appropriate will, or who become incapacitated but have no trusted, well-briefed attorney to look after your affairs. The aim of this book is to help you ensure that the time of your passing does not involve a lot of unnecessary stress for those you leave behind; that your assets end up with the people you wanted them to go to; and that your estate is not frittered away on pointless expenses like legal wrangles or paying unnecessary tax.

But the fact remains that we will all die at some stage, and the better we can prepare for it, the better the outcome should be for everybody. I often suggest that people withdraw their money from superannuation when their death is imminent to avoid the death tax. Their response is usually, "How does anybody know when their death is imminent?" While that may be true in a literal sense, less than 1% of the 190,000 annual deaths in Australia happen suddenly. Most people have at least three months' notice.

There is a wide range of possibilities. You may be told you have a terminal disease with possibly five years to live, or you may be given just three months to live — you may suffer something that leaves you seriously incapacitated and still live for years. There are also thousands of people who are now in aged care, where the average stay is 18 months before they pass on. So, most people do have some notice — this chapter covers the things you should be looking at when you know your death is getting closer.

A doctor friend tells me that often the last thing people want to think about when they are told death is imminent is their financial affairs. But it's important to focus on the entire situation — items not dealt with can cause horrendous problems for the family after death.

Be prepared, do your best to expect the unexpected, and you can leave a valuable legacy when you go.

A READER'S TALE

You never know what life is going to throw at you and this is never truer than when you are older.

My parents were in their late 80s and early 90s and in good health for their age and living independently with only a small amount of help.

Then they weren't! For the next four years we were dealing with all the complexities, costs and paperwork of the health, retirement village and aged care systems and then, sadly, the management of their estates, as they died eight months apart.

We were so grateful that they had their own financial adviser, accountant and solicitor, with a financial plan in place, as we traversed so many changes in their individual requirements.

The things we learned from our experiences that we didn't realise before were:

- We had always seen our parents' living needs as a couple, but once their health declined at different times they became independent individuals who needed very different care and living requirements.
- The more conversations you can have with your family about your life and death wishes, the easier it is for everyone to bring those wishes to making all the decisions that have to be made, especially when your health and capacity decline.
- Get as much professional advice and knowledge as you can; the paperwork can become overwhelming, and your most important job at this time is to stay focused on them and their care.

Grieving

People usually think of grief as something that begins after someone dies, and in many ways that is true. But when people know they are dying, it is absolutely normal for both they themselves and those around them to start grieving at once. Grief is generally acknowledged to be a process, and one that people experience in many different ways.

Those leaving

Living to your 70s, 80s, 90s or even your 100s is no guarantee that you will feel ready to go. If you don't want to move on, you may try to avoid your feelings by refusing to prepare for the inevitable.

In contrast, if you feel that you've had a good life and it may be time to leave it, taking care of those you leave behind can be very appealing. Whatever you may feel, if you know that death is approaching — and it is life's one great certainty — we urge you to look for some way to motivate yourself to help those you will be leaving behind.

Those left behind

It is well known that the best way to handle grief is to express your emotions and get it out of your system. However, we live in a culture where many people, especially males, believe it is wrong to cry in public and as a result do not gain the benefits of grieving.

My mother died suddenly at age 54, when I was 21. As I was the oldest child, it fell to me to look after the rest of the family. Consequently, I never went through the grieving process — I was too busy taking care of the others. In any event, I thought it was weak to show how badly I was hurt by her death. The result was that for the next 33 years I started crying whenever I thought about her, and it was only when I finally allowed myself to pour out my emotions at a counselling session in 1994 that I became able to handle her death, which had taken place so long ago.

The funeral process is often a time of grief but it is also an opportunity to hasten the grieving process and so speed the healing process. Feel free to express what you feel. If you don't do it then, you will probably have to do it later.

A READER'S TALE

My wife died suddenly seven months ago. I am still grieving and I am reliably told it will take at least 12 months — maybe 24 — to come to terms with the loss. I have found a book, *Have you met my grief?* by Jodie Atkinson, very comforting. She went through the same experience of the death of her husband and could not find a good resource to deal with it, so she wrote a book. It deals with her feelings and tries to normalise the experience for the reader. I have found her book far better than clinical psychologists (who I am also seeing), who have the sympathy but lack the empathy.

Anger is a common stage of grieving, and if you are left to deal with a mess, you may well feel angry with the person who died and dropped you into the situation. That's a tricky place to be, because not only do you have the practical problems, you also have strong emotions to deal with that you — and people around you — may consider unacceptable. All we can say here is that you are not alone if you find yourself facing this dilemma, and that there are people you can turn to, to help with both the emotional and practical aspects of what you are going through. Remember that, while it may feel as if you are alone, this is actually quite a common situation.

Leaving a legacy

Many people are keen to leave a legacy. They figure it's pointless to go through life having all sorts of experiences, and achieving many goals, for it all to vanish on the day they die.

One form of legacy is living a life that leaves a mark on the world. There are so many ways you could do this. You could start a business, raise a family, be active in charitable organisations, give help and support generously within your community, or be a leader in your field. George Bernard Shaw expressed this idea in words that have become very well known:

> *Life is no brief candle to me. It is a sort of splendid torch which I have got hold of for the moment, and I want to make it burn as brightly as possible before handing it on to future generations.*

There are many ways of leaving a legacy. In this section we will talk briefly about documenting your life, donating to a worthy cause in such a way that the benefits flow down to future generations, and helping your children and grandchildren to have a better life, which are just a few of the most common legacies. It's really up to you.

Documenting your life

One way of documenting your life, which is becoming increasingly common, is to record your life story as an audio or even video. To do this, you simply sit in front of a recording device, armed with some notes about your life, and speak about your impressions of what happened at key points in your life. You may want to talk about when you started school, when you met your true love, or some of the challenges and successes in raising a family or starting a business. I think it's great to include some of the lessons you have learned on your journey through life. Some families play part of the recording at your funeral. One of the best things about this is that people get to hear the words spoken by the person themselves.

Although I'm quite used to writing, I used a life writing package that sent me a weekly question — How did you get your first job? What were your favourite children's stories? Where did you go on holidays as a child? What was your first boss like? Of course, you could do it all yourself, but the questions were great triggers, and often generated more questions. I typed my responses and sent them back, keeping a copy for myself. By the end of the year I had a 40,000 word document, already roughly collated into a book.

This particular package offered a year's worth of story prompts, some handy ways to share the stories with other people, and one or more hardcover books with black and white pages and a full colour cover. There was no hard sell, and I thought it was good value, given the benefit I got from using it.

A philanthropic legacy

Most taxpayers are familiar with the income tax deductions available for charitable giving, and around 30% of taxpayers claim a deduction each year. Giving while living brings the joy of seeing the positive impact of your generosity.

Some people — particularly those uncertain about their future living needs and the cost of care — instead choose to leave gifts to charities in their will. While the tax concessions are not as generous, let me share some of the lesser known tax incentives for charitable giving on death.

Capital gains tax (CGT) exemption

This is available for some bequests in wills. It can help maximise the value of bequests to the community through a more tax-effective distribution of a deceased estate.

CGT is normally imposed on the profits gained from selling or transferring certain assets, such as property and shares, that have increased in capital value. When these assets are inherited by Australian individuals, they inherit both the asset and its cost base, so the beneficiaries will ultimately pay the full CGT on sale. (There is an exception here for assets acquired by the deceased before the introduction of CGT in 1985; in these circumstances the cost base is reset to the value of the asset on the date of death.)

However, if the beneficiary is a charity endorsed as a deductible gift recipient (DGR) at the time of the donor's death, then CGT is neither paid by the estate nor by the beneficiary.

You can therefore maximise your bequest to the community and achieve a more tax-effective outcome by directing a gift of assets carrying a large capital gain, such as shares, to one or more of the 30,000+ DGR charities in Australia.

Note that charitable structures created under the terms of your will do not qualify for the exemption, because they did not have DGR status at the time of your death.

Other assets in your estate can be used to fulfil other provisions you want to make to family, friends and other organisations. This clearly requires a bit of forward planning and careful discussion with an estate planning lawyer.

Tax-deductible donations to a public ancillary fund

A donation made before 30 June is a great way to reduce or eliminate a capital gain.

If you sold an investment property for $1.2 million that triggered a capital gain of $800,000, application of the 50% discount would reduce the taxable gain to $400,000. And if you made a tax-deductible donation to charity of $400,000, the entire taxable capital gain would be wiped out.

Now I appreciate that many people may be hesitant about donating $400,000 in a lump sum. So, use a public ancillary fund, like the Australian Philanthropic Services Foundation. You get the benefits of an immediate tax deduction, but the fund invests your money, and you can then direct it to pay out to charities of your choice over the coming years. Your fund must donate at least 4% of the balance every year. This is what my wife and I do.

The donations we've made over the years are set aside in our own named giving fund, and each year at least 4% of the balance is given to charities that we support. Because the funds are invested and the returns are tax-free, while we are actively giving money to charity, the amount we can give is also growing. Future directions for charitable distributions after you pass can be left with your kids or grandkids, or through a clear statement of wishes specifying the charities or causes that you would like to support through the public ancillary fund.

As the money in the foundation starts to grow, you can get all the family members involved deciding where your gifts should be directed. The funds should be earning at least 6% per annum, so if you stipulate that the required minimum 4% per annum is the most to be spent each year, you ensure the fund grows in perpetuity and should provide benefits until infinity. It's a fantastic legacy to leave behind you, and it's wonderful to get the children and grandkids involved.

I suggest you develop a family policy as to where the gifts should go. We've decided that every gift we give must help people through the generations. Each year we sponsor one student to a university. This gives a good education to somebody who would have no chance of getting it without the sponsorship. That doesn't just change their life — it also changes the lives of their descendants.

We are also keen to sponsor charities helping people escape domestic violence — we figure if we can help kids escape a bad home life, it works down the line. Doing this with your family is very satisfying, and encourages a sense of charity in them.

Helping the kids

Giving or lending money to your children at times when they most need it, instead of waiting until you are 90 and they are 65 can be another good option. Many parents are taking the view that it's best to help their children get a start early in life, and watch them enjoy it.

These days, the bank of mum and dad is one of the top mortgage lenders in Australia. The average home today costs around eight times average earnings, whereas in the 1970s it was more like 2.6 times. So there is no doubt that buying a home is much more difficult for young people now than it was 30 years ago.

I have long been of the "help sooner rather than later" view on one proviso — it must be a hand up, not a handout. We insist that the children, and grandchildren, demonstrate that they are responsible financial managers before any funds are handed over, which means making sure they are not tied down by credit card debt or personal loans. Some parents match the children's contributions, for example, giving $1000 for every $1000 they save for a home deposit.

But if you hand over a lump sum, is it going to be a gift or a loan? Apart from wanting to help their children, parents often fret about what will happen if their children have a relationship breakdown. If the money is handed over as a gift, might your child's partner walk out the door with half of the money you've given them?

My wife and I have long believed that "a gift given is a gift given" and it is best to give money to our children on a non-recourse basis. As far as we are concerned, the grief that would be caused all round by a divorce would be so horrendous that fighting about ways to claw back financial assistance that may have been given years ago is a bridge too far.

If there is a clear understanding that the monies are to be repaid, a simple loan agreement would be in order. This should include terms such as repayment frequency and interest.

However, there is a time limit to consider — each state has its own *Limitations of Actions Act* however, generally speaking, if no repayments have been made for six years from the date of the loan, the loan cannot be enforced. Repayments and a loan agreement are the best way to evidence an intention that the monies are a loan.

Families are often shocked when a parent dies to discover a loan to an adult child is not enforceable as the loan was made more than six years ago, there is no formal agreement and no repayments have been made, despite the parent clearly stating in their will that the loan is not forgiven. In family law proceedings, the court needs to be satisfied that it is a genuine loan, evidenced by an agreement and regular repayments.

Be careful if you intend to apply for the pension. Assets given away five years or more before application for the pension cease to exist for Centrelink purposes. If you make a gift and not a loan, you may boost your age pension.

Hypothetical: Your last 18 months

For the purposes of this exercise let's assume that you have been told you have a terminal illness and may well die within the next 18 months. These are the things that need to be considered.

Plan for your funeral

Discussing the funeral might be a good starting point. It allows open dialogue between family members and gives you the freedom to think about how you would like your funeral to be.

I recommend the book *Never Forgotten* by Michelle Lagana. It's only available on Kindle as far as I know, but goes into great depth as to things you might like to think about. It contains a huge amount of information and even includes suggestions for who the pallbearers might be and ideas for preparation of the funeral booklet.

At this stage, think about whether there are any funeral arrangements already in place. These could include a funeral bond or a pre-payment. If they are in place, it is important they be recorded and the documents readily available. The whole family should know of their existence; the last thing they need is to walk out of the service and discover the funeral had already been paid for with a different undertaker.

Share precious personal items

Often people have a range of belongings that really aren't appropriate to mention in the will, but which have considerable sentimental value. These may include photo albums, DVDs, family heirlooms, jewellery, kitchenware such as plates and glasses, or even items like workshop equipment or clothing.

The months before dying could be a time for reminiscing with family and friends, and a great opportunity as you give them some of these items, though remember this may trigger a CGT event, see pages 170–172.

Share important contacts

Most households require a team of people to make it function. These could include your plumber, electrician, gardener, bank staff, solicitor and various healthcare professionals. List the roles and contact details for all these people so things can carry on after your death.

Get your documents in order

It's absolutely vital that the necessary documents are up-to-date and readily available. We discussed this in depth in Chapter 4, and let me remind you about the appendix, Keeping the right records. It includes a link to the ***Executors' and attorneys' cheat sheet***, which is available to download, complete, save, share as appropriate, and update at any time.

Is there a will, an enduring power of attorney (EPA) and an advance care directive? Are these documents up-to-date and readily available to the family? True, the EPA ends on your death but if you lose capacity — or just the desire — to deal with practical matters as time passes, the EPA could be essential for a range of financial and medical matters. You can probably figure out where you are likely to need the EPA. If you're not sure, I suggest you take it to at least your bank, accountant, and financial adviser, and have them vet it long before it's needed. I have heard numerous instances of people turning up with an EPA at the last minute, only for the institution to find some reason to reject it, or say they need a week to approve it.

Take a close look at your will. Have there been any major changes to your assets since you made the will? What about the beneficiaries: look for any changes in their situation since the will was executed. These could include having more children, changing tax brackets or ending a long-term relationship. In any such cases, the will should be urgently reviewed in light of their changed circumstances.

Talk to your executor/s

It is your executor/s who will manage your estate after you pass. It would be great if you could meet with them sooner rather than later to discuss your affairs in depth, and give them an idea of how you would like things managed after you die. This will not just help them do their job, but also give you some comfort, knowing how your estate will be managed.

Sort out your super

If you have superannuation, you should share the recent statements and explain it all to your family. If your super includes life insurance, that will need to be noted, and your will may need to be amended if a large sum is expected to be paid to the estate. Are trustee nominations to be used? Are any binding death benefit nominations up to date? Are they lapsing or non-lapsing? All of this information is easily obtainable on the superannuation fund website or by calling your superannuation provider.

If you have an SMSF the most recent set of accounts should be available for the family to see, and you should introduce them to the people who administer the fund. This may be the family accountant or a specialist administration firm.

Remember the death tax of 15% plus Medicare levy, which is levied on taxable superannuation payments made to a non-dependant. You may want to withdraw as much of your super as you can before death and place that in your bank account, or, if you have enough liquidity, in a joint account your EPA and executor can access to cover your costs when your bank accounts are frozen.

Clarify the finances

In many couples, one person tends to manage the finances; when they die, problems can arise for the survivor. If you are approaching death, you will need to teach whoever will take over from you how your bank accounts work and give access to all email and contacts so things can be carried on or closed down when you have gone.

This is also a good time to introduce your stockbroker and financial adviser to the people taking over from you, and make sure they are right across your whole portfolio. Time spent discussing your investments, the reasons why they were made, and their potential is time well spent.

Check with your accountant if there are any changes you should make before you pass, such as selling assets with a capital gain to make use of any existing capital losses before they cease to exist on your death.

Delegate digital assets

Ensure that you have put in place the appropriate delegations for your online accounts to enable another person to access your accounts to operate, close, or delete them. Make sure someone is aware of all your online accounts, including social media, email, payment portals, and any other presence you have online. Although these accounts are usually not transferable (as they are not the property of the deceased), many enable the account-holder to appoint another person to deal with the account on their death.

Loyalty programs and points are often not transferable after death (they usually revert back to the provider); however, it is sometimes possible to transfer these points during your lifetime to another family member. This could be particularly valuable if you have a credit card linked to an airline frequent flyer program with hundreds of thousands of points. A little forward thinking could provide a family member with enough points for an overseas trip after your death.

If you have cryptocurrency or are trading online, make sure the appropriate delegations or authorities have been put in place to enable these accounts to be closed.

Consider any issues arising from your current situation

If you are single, who will take care of a much-loved pet?

If you are partnered, does your partner have special needs, and if so, how will they be cared for when you are gone? A common situation with older people is that one person becomes the other's carer, and the situation can get very difficult if it's the carer who dies.

If you have children, will they be able to do the things that normally fall to family? If not, or if you have no children to call on, who will take on responsibilities like going through all your belongings and advising people of your passing?

Do you hold a life interest in a property? If so, what details do you need to give your executor to enable them to hand the property back to the original estate?

Is your current name different from a previous name? If so, what does your executor need to know about your earlier name/s, and what paperwork will they need to demonstrate that they can act for you under that name?

End note

"Putting your affairs in order" is a term that is commonly used when people are approaching the end of their life. As this book has illustrated, it is not as easy as it sounds. However it should not be overwhelming, or consume all of your spare time.

Consider setting aside some time for a general overview of the issues covered in this book. It could be as simple as finding your current will and reading the section on wills. Then perhaps find your power of attorney and do the same. Take small steps. Write a to-do list. Enlist some help, whether it be family, friends, an accountant or your solicitor. You can share the workload.

Losing a loved one is never easy, but losing a loved one and dealing with a disorganised estate adds another layer of stress upon the existing grief. Nobody wants to leave that for their family. Ensure that part of your legacy is an organised estate.

Appendix: Keeping the right records

Keeping the right records where the right people can find them is an important part of estate planning. As you have read, missing or wrongly executed documents can cause major headaches when someone else has to deal with your affairs. There are a range of measures to tackle this problem, and this section gives you some ideas.

Remember that some people are much more detail-minded than others. My goal is to keep this basic guide as simple as possible; a more comprehensive approach is supported by the BAN TACS package. I have also included a brief guide to what you need to provide your digital executor.

A basic guide

The vital records

It is absolutely worth storing your vital documents in a fireproof document safe at home. There's a wide range of these safes available, at various prices, from hardware shops and locksmiths.

There are three key documents, which must be valid and up-to-date:

- will
- enduring power of attorney
- advance care directive.

The will is best kept at the office of the solicitor where it was signed. You should have a certified copy at home as well.

The other two documents may be needed often. Your solicitor can keep the originals and provide you with certified copies, or you can keep them in your home for easy access.

For each family member, you should also have:

- birth certificates
- marriage certificates
- proof of ID for the executor, if they are a family member, e.g. a passport
- an up-to-date list of your beneficiaries' contact details.

Having these available will speed up probate and make administering your will much easier.

You are welcome to use the ***Executors' and attorneys' cheat sheet***, which is free to download from my website. This is a fillable form, allowing you to enter and save a wide range of information on your computer. A printed copy should be kept in the fireproof safe with the other documents. It includes vital information such as where your will is kept and who are the executors of your will. There's also room for much more information if you choose to put it there. It is designed as the primary document to let your executors know how to proceed. What follows are some tips to make your record keeping simpler and more effective.

Records for your home

The executor's first main jobs will be to pay outstanding bills and cancel items such as monthly streaming services, tolls, and club memberships. Then they will need to deal with utilities and insurances, which may need to continue to be paid, moved into a new account-holder's name, or cancelled.

In our home, we find the most effective way to handle this is to just have a manila folder marked "Home", in which we put all items that are not tax-deductible. This includes the latest paid rates notices for the family home, electricity and gas bills, insurance bills and every other household item that will need attention once you pass on.

Superannuation

Self-managed superannuation funds must prepare an annual statement of accounts, which you will need to keep on file.

If you are a member of a regular superannuation fund you will receive at least one statement each financial year, which gives all the details you need, including your member number, your balance, and any life insurance in the fund. Keep this on file.

You should have a separate superannuation folder for all these documents. If you have multiple superannuation funds, make sure this is clear in your record keeping.

Records for your investments

If you have assets such as shares or investment properties, records need to be kept (to minimise capital gains tax) until the assets are disposed of. If you have ever been an overseas resident for tax purposes, your executor will even need to know these dates to calculate the 50% CGT discount.

Property

We find having a folder for each property works brilliantly — just like the home folder. Documents for all expenses connected with that property are in one place; these are useful for the accountant each year when tax time arrives, and also provide full details for an executor or attorney.

Listed shares

If you buy listed shares direct, you will receive regular dividend statements, and every time you buy or sell a share you will receive a CHESS (clearing house electronic subregister system) statement posted to your home address. These are a great record of your transactions, even though they do not include the price.

Give each share its own manila folder, and keep both dividend and CHESS statements.

If you use a stockbroker, they will probably have a system that records all the shares you own, with all the relevant details. This is usually the case with wrap accounts (such as Macquarie Wrap, Hub, Acclaim, Morgans Wealth and Panorama BT). In this case, you just need to record which stockbroker or wrap account you are using on the ***Executors' and attorneys' cheat sheet***.

Unlisted assets

These include managed funds and property syndicates. Because they are unlisted, they cannot simply be sold on the market: to redeem or transfer money you need to deal with the manager.

These assets will send an annual tax statement, and an additional statement of investments on request. If you keep all these, it should be simple for the executor to communicate with the manager. Remember to document your cost base too, as there is no guarantee the asset manager will know it.

Passwords

Most financial transactions are now made online, and there may not even be a paper record. It will be much easier for your executor — or attorney or lawyer — to find out what you have and owe if they can get into your accounts online.

There are two ways to share your passwords.

1. **On paper:** Write down your passwords and instructions on a piece of paper and keep them in the fireproof safe with your other estate planning documents. Of course, this relies on you to keep the sheet updated.
2. **In a password manager:** How they do it varies, but digital password managers offer fully encrypted ways to share passwords with specified people, or give them the ability to log in without actually knowing your password. Most also offer some kind of digital legacy arrangement for when you pass away.

A comprehensive guide

The BAN TACS ***Getting your affairs in order*** package is a comprehensive resource where you can place all your financial information. You are also prompted to scan relevant documents, which remain linked to the spreadsheets and easily accessible. Having all this information in an electronic format enables you to share it easily and securely with the people who need to know.

For a one-off fee, you get a set of spreadsheets with clear instructions on how you can get your affairs in great order. ***www.bantacs.com.au/shop-2/getting-your-affairs-in-order-made-simple/***
Remember to type "Noel" into the voucher section of the shopping cart for a 20% discount.

Digital assets

These days our online presence holds a surprising amount of value. From cherished photos to cryptocurrency holdings, neglecting digital assets in your estate plan can create a tangled mess for your loved ones. Here's how to ensure your online legacy is handled smoothly.

1. **Take inventory:** Start by listing your digital assets. This includes:
   - email accounts
   - social media profiles
   - online financial accounts (including crypto wallets)

- cloud storage services
- domain names and websites.

If you use a password manager, this really just amounts to making sure that all your digital assets are in it.

If you are recording this manually, you will have to figure out how to keep it secure, as you will need to include:

- usernames
- passwords
- any key details, such as customer numbers, if these are different from usernames, and cPanel details for domain names.

2. **Decide their fate:** Most digital assets cannot be passed on like a house. Some platforms allow ownership of digital content to be transferred, while others have specific closure procedures. Ideally, determine what you want done with each account; such as memorials for social media accounts or deletion requests for sensitive information.

3. **Appoint a digital executor:** Don't assume your legal executor will have the technical know-how to navigate all your online accounts. Choose a tech-savvy and trustworthy individual to manage your digital assets, and check that they agree to do this for you. Then ensure they will be provided with your list and instructions when the time is right.

4. **Secure instructions:** Never include passwords directly in another document, such as your will. Instead create a separate, secure document outlining access information and instructions for each account. Store this securely, accessible to your digital executor but separate from your will.

5. **Communicate clearly:** Inform both your legal and digital executors about your plans. Let them know where to find the records they will need, how to communicate with each other, and ensure they understand your wishes.

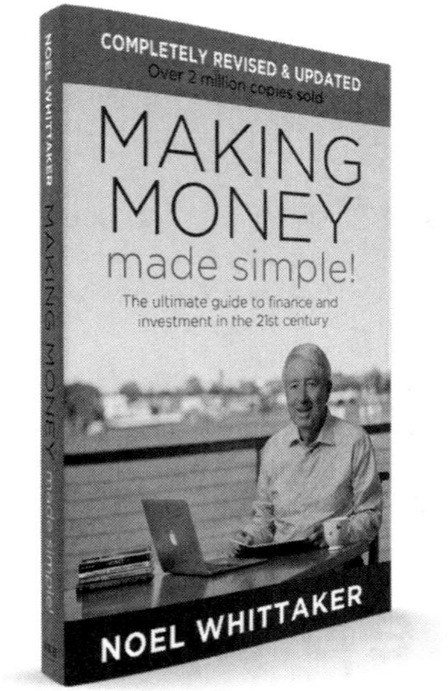

This is the most successful and influential of all Noel's books. *Making Money Made Simple* smashed sales records and sold over a million copies around the world. It stayed on the bestsellers list for a record nine years, and was voted in the Top 100 of the Most Influential Books of the 20th Century.

After a recent update, *Making Money Made Simple* is back better than ever to teach you the essentials of money, investment, borrowing and personal finance in the way that only Noel knows how.

Retirement can be a jungle of decision-making

What to invest in? How long will your money last? Are you eligible for any age pension? Is downsizing right for you? How much should you spend now, and how much would you like to leave to your kids? Add the challenges of finding the right advice, understanding new products, estate planning, volatile markets, unexpected events such as GFC and COVID-19, and continual changes to our tax, superannuation, age pension and aged care regulations … Above all, how do you value and nurture your greatest assets — your health and your relationships?

In the simple style for which Noel is renowned, this book covers all the key aspects of retirement, and will become your indispensable guide on what we hope will be a happy, healthy and prosperous retirement.

Will the aged pension meet your needs? It's unlikely. That's why you MUST think seriously about superannuation. It isn't as confusing as you might think.

In *Superannuation Made Simple*, Noel Whittaker unravels the mysteries of superannuation and shows you how to use the system to grow your retirement funds faster.

The perfect gift for a young person

The Beginner'$ Guide to Wealth is much more than a simple introduction to finance; it also focuses on building the skills to make money in this rapidly changing world.

In this book — co-authored with son James Whittaker — Noel teaches young people how to get going, how to increase their income and how to invest their money when they start to make it.

Index